It is my prayer
that this little book bless
you, and bring great glory
to our Lord, King Jesus

Christopher Gosnell VJ

The PROBLEM *with* CHRIST

Why we don't understand Jesus, His enemies, or the early church.

CHRISTOPHER GORTON

ISBN-13: 978-1490439051

DEDICATION

To the memory of
Matthew Garber

and his Lord
–the King Jesus.

He came to learn;
instead he taught.
The good fight,
indeed he fought.
We shall not speak,
by our King's choosing,
until like Him
we win by losing.

"Safe?" said Mr. Beaver; "don't you hear what Mrs. Beaver tells you? Who said anything about safe? 'Course he isn't safe. But he's good. He's the King, I tell you."

– C.S. LEWIS, THE LION, THE WITCH, AND THE WARDROBE

Table of Contents

Every Thought Captive

"For though we walk in the flesh, we do not war according to the flesh, for the weapons of our warfare are not of the flesh, but divinely powerful for the destruction of fortresses. We are destroying speculations and every lofty thing raised up against the knowledge of God, and we are taking every thought captive to the obedience of Christ." – II Corinthians 10:3-5

If you were deceived, how would you know it?

It is not without reason that the scriptures refer to our enemy as "the deceiver." Deception is his most powerful and most used weapon, and unfortunately, the one which we seem the least prepared to deal with. Dealing with deception is made difficult by the fact that, by its very definition, its victims are unaware of their deceived condition.

Nobody ever really thinks they are wrong. This is not necessarily arrogance, it is simply a result of our own logic. I know that I certainly do not want to believe untruth, and that if I find an error in my thinking I proceed to change it. You think the same way. Nobody wants to be wrong—therefore we all think that we are right![1]

Of course, because we know arrogance is not a Christian trait, we don't unapologetically declare that we are right. Instead, we make it clear that we do not know everything, and that, doubtless, some of what we believe is in error. Yet, when we are pressed on specifics, we discover our unconscious belief in our own inerrancy!

For the Christian, this whole problem of belief versus deception is compounded by the fact that we admittedly "walk by faith and not by sight."[2] We rightly steel ourselves against the onslaught of ungodly errors that society hurls at us, and while we may not have ready answers for the seemingly intellectual arguments a materialist might raise, we rest in faith that our God did, indeed, create the heavens, the earth, the seas, and all that they contain. Unfortunately, this can lead to an inappropriate inflexibility when we confuse genuine biblical teaching with erroneous presuppositions. An example of this can be seen in those whose proper respect for the divinely inspired Bible becomes inappropriately

---

1 I am speaking of cognitive and not moral error here. Hopefully, we recognize that in our battle with sinful behavior we all have room for improvement and can indeed point to specific areas in which we are in need of assistance. (This is not to say that there is not an interplay in both directions between cognitive and moral error.)

2 II Corinthians 5:7

attached to a particular system of theology.

Even more insidious are cultural biases that blind us to clear biblical teaching, and reinterpret them in ways that destroy the authors' intent. For example, consider the hermeneutic of the southern slave owners of America's antebellum south, many of who claimed to be (and presumably truly were trying to be) followers of Jesus. In the biblical instructions concerning the treatment of slaves, they found divine approval of the practice of slavery, rather than a limitation of its evils.[3]

It is important to remember that these cultural biases do not exist solely in secular society, but also within churches and denominations. It was these chains of blindness that bound the people of Israel, and for which Jesus had the least tolerance. Those who were bound by failure and who recognized their moral poverty received Jesus' mercy, while those who nullified the effect of God's word by their systemic re-interpretation earned His harshest words.

They were not simply in error—they were deceived. Error, while it may be corporate, is essentially a one-sided affair. Deception, on the other hand is two-sided; there exists the deceived, and the deceiver. It implies that an advantage accrues to the deceiver at the expense of the deceived. The

---

3 I hope that I will not scare you off by pointing out that there is not one example in the New Testament where wives are told to be submissive to their husbands that the immediate context does not include similar instruction to slaves concerning their masters! The normative instruction is that we submit to one another as servants of our King.

active work of the deceiver ensures that deception is more difficult to escape than simple error or ignorance. The latter two may be overcome by simple education, often with no more consequence than simple embarrassment. Deception is much more difficult to overcome because it is actively maintained—not to mention that we face a deceptive enemy who is capable of placing first-person thoughts into our minds, an enemy our residual fallen nature is in cahoots with. The habits of mind and body that we learned before coming to our King only reinforce his deception.

How might we escape?

First of all, we need to recognize that God gives more light to those who respond to the light they have already received. In affluent societies such as ours it is disturbing to see the extent to which those who claim to follow Jesus refuse to walk in radical (basic) obedience to His guidance. Re-read the gospels, noting His economic teachings and consider 1 John 2:6: "The one who says he abides in Him ought himself to walk in the same manner as He walked." Refusal to grow in obedience on these most basic, clear, and indisputable fronts is a sure recipe for opening the door to the enemy's deception.

Next to obedience to the things you already understand, becoming a servant is the first and foremost way to show God you are ready for more light. For instance, ask God to show you someone in your life who is difficult to love, and then seek ways to help that person see God's love in your behavior toward them. Third, ask the Holy Spirit to reveal to you any area in which you are deceived. It may be that a "strong man" has taken over and you are a prisoner in your own house—pray that you be set free and that he be bound. Be forewarned, God has promised to deliver us from our enemies, not our friends! It is likely that if you are deceived, your enemy has ensured that you are very comfortable in that state. Rest assured that, if you are deceived, he will see to it that you are unaware of the deception and will enlist your participation in resisting any attempt at enlightenment.

This brings us to the subject at hand. You are about to turn the page in a book[4] that may also be the turning of a metaphorical page of your life. Based on previous experience, I feel quite certain the enemy will try to convince you that what you are reading is not revealing deception, but is itself an attempt to deceive you. That may be true! I seriously suggest that you pause right now and pray; seek God's counsel as to whether or not you should continue; and if so, petition both His protection and wisdom to recognize the truth and the courage to act on it.

---

4 Please understand that this is the first in a series of works which is far from complete, regarding the history and theology of the kingdom of God, with significant emphasis on biblical cosmology and spiritual warfare. Comments, questions, and corrections are welcome and encouraged by the author. He can be contacted via his blog: RadicalFish.net

I will begin by presenting a simple fact—one that can be easily confirmed. It is my prayer that the realization of the church's (and maybe your) ignorance of that surprising fact will be the alarm that wakes her (and you) to the awareness of a great deception that the enemy has used to turn her into a zombie in his service on the world stage.

Chapter one introduces you to the main idea this book presents. Chapters two and three provide evidence to support that idea, and chapters four and five analyze how this idea impacts our understanding of the scriptures and our Christian perspectives. If you find yourself getting bogged down in chapter two or three, rather than set the book aside, I encourage you to just skip ahead to the next chapter, and return to what you skipped later.

You will be tempted to dismiss what I present as a simple piece of trivia, but I submit it is a key that unlocks the purpose and power of God in this age. Who has not read the book of Acts and wondered why we do not see such things today? I make a bold claim—we have been deceived; we do not know clearly what we have been saved from—or for!

Proceed in His favor, secure in His love, with eyes wide open, seeking His Truth.

Favor and peace in Him Whom we serve,
    Christopher Gorton

One

THE PROBLEM WITH "CHRIST"

"In religion and politics, people's beliefs and convictions are in almost every case gotten at second hand, and without examination" —MARK TWAIN

"Half of writing history is hiding the truth."
—CAPT. MALCOLM REYNOLDS, *SERENITY*

This chapter's title sounds heretical, I know.

But before you make that judgment, please read further. First of all, let me clearly state that I am convinced of the authenticity of Jesus of Nazareth, as recorded in the New Testament. I also believe that He is, in fact, the King of Kings and Lord of Lords, that He was raised physically from the dead, and that He will return to judge the living and the dead.

Nonetheless, I have come to believe there is a significant problem with *Christ*—not the Person, but the title itself.

7

In fact, I believe that the problem is so serious that I have personally concluded that those who claim to truly follow Him should no longer use the term, other than in special and limited circumstances. So, if you have the patience, read on to discover what has brought me to that conclusion.

Meanwhile, an example may help clarify my point. There are many Christians today who take strong exception to the use of the term *Xmas* when referring in writing—or even worse, in speaking—of Christmas. On the other hand, those who use the term often maintain that they are only using a long, time-honored church tradition—abbreviating the Greek word for Christ (Χριστός), only using the first letter to represent the whole word. Those who oppose the use of Xmas, however, maintain that, whatever *X* might have stood for in the past, today it is universally used in its algebraic sense to stand for an unknown. All the arguments in its favor, they maintain, are simply an excuse to remove one more vestige of Christian influence from an increasingly secularized society.

Personally, I have come to see this controversy as something of a "tempest in a teapot," designed to distract us from more pressing issues, such as the problem with the word *Christ*. If someone opposes the use of *Xmas,* I can only point out that, in some sense, even *Christ* has become an *X* in its own right—a title that has been stripped of its original meaning and made so nondescript and impotent as to lose its usefulness.

The fact of the matter is, the world is already ignorant of Him, as is Christianity itself, in a large measure. (I am simply using the word Christianity here in reference to those who call themselves Christians.)

While the Holy Spirit has indeed shed abroad the truth of "Christ" in the hearts of His followers, He has often done so without recourse to the first-century clarity of the word *Christ* itself. I hope to show you that, for almost 1,700 years, we've replaced the truth of "Christ" with another *X*—namely the word *Christ*!

So, what does *Christ* mean?

For several years, I have been asking individuals and groups this question, and have been dismayed to find no one that could give an answer that I felt was correct. At first I was tempted to believe—as you may be tempted now—that this was proof of my supreme arrogance, and/or self-delusion. This seemed far more likely than the possibility that the essential meaning of the central word of our faith, and the source of our identity as believers, could have been stolen from us long ago.

That said, I have been comforted by the fact that most people realized right away that they had no idea what *Christ* meant, and that they had simply resorted to guessing. (Typically, guesses included Savior, Blessed, Crucified, God, or even the last name of Jesus.) When they heard what follows, they were in joyous agreement. (For any scholars reading this, I should point out that the answer is not merely "messiah," nor "anointed," but please keep reading...)

It needs to be emphasized here that we are not speaking of new truths. The Holy Spirit has already convinced you of the essential meaning of the word *Christ* if you are truly His follower; it is simply that God has allowed the enemy an apparent victory in rendering the word void of significance. By God's grace, you will soon see how this happened, and why I make the ridiculous sounding claim that true followers of "the Christ" should no longer use the term.

A DISTURBING DISCOVERY

Before sharing the solution to this puzzle, I should also share how I became aware of it. Some years ago the Lord led me, with my family, to abandon a successful career as a science teacher and move to Costa Rica to be salt and light in a small rural community. Obviously, one of our first priorities there was to learn Spanish in order to communicate the gospel—and to buy groceries and find the bathroom. To this end, I determined to start doing my personal Bible reading in Spanish, and obtained a Bible that had Spanish and English columns side by side. This proved to be an incredible blessing, not only in advancing my Spanish, but also in understanding the Word.

One day I was reading in John chapter one, and noticed something strange. Many of you may not have access to a Spanish/English Bible, so I have reproduced the selection below. You will find the four pertinent verses reproduced with the important sections in boldface and italics. Please read over both sections; you should not need to understand Spanish to see what I observed.

San Juan 1

38 Jesús se volvió, y viendo que le seguían, les dijo*: ¿Qué buscáis? Y ellos le dijeron: *__Rabí__ (que traducido quiere decir, __Maestro__)*, ¿dónde te hospedas? 41 El encontró* primero a su hermano Simón, y le dijo*: Hemos hallado *al __Mesías__ (que traducido quiere decir, __Cristo__)*.

John 1

38 And Jesus turned and saw them following, and said to them*, "What do you seek?" They said to Him, "*__Rabbi__ (which translated means __Teacher__)*, where are You staying?" 41 He found* first his own brother Simon and said* to him, "We have found *the __Messiah__" (which translated means __Christ__)*.

Did you see it? Great; but if not, go back and read just the emphasized phrases, paying special attention to the four pairs of underlined words. I had probably read this passage in English a hundred times, but had never seen what I now saw. Even now I only saw it because I had the English and Spanish versions side by side. There is a profound asymmetry in the first two pairs of underlined words, compared to the second pair. Please note the pairs:

Spanish Bible		English Bible	
Rabi	**Maestro**	**Rabbi**	**Teacher**
Transliterated Aramaic	Spanish word	Transliterated Aramaic	English word
Mesias	**Cristo**	**Messiah**	**Christ**
Transliterated Aramaic	Transliterated Greek!	Transliterated Aramaic	Transliterated Greek!

Once the significance of this asymmetry is understood, the implications are stunning. The first word of each pair, in both Spanish and English, (columns one and three), are almost identical. This is because these words have been transliterated out of Aramaic[5] into Greek by John, and modern translators continue this practice to accurately portray what he was trying to express. (*Transliteration* is when a word is changed from one language to conform to the characters, pronunciation and/or spelling norms of another.)

The second word in each pair should be the translation of the first, so in the second and fourth columns we should find very different words. In the top row this is the case, but then something goes awry. In this chart, what one would expect to find paired with *Mesias*, or Messiah, would be a Spanish or English word. Instead, what we find is a transliteration of a Greek word: Χριστός, (*christos*), Cristo in Spanish and Christ in English. They both bear striking similarity to the

---

5 Aramaic is a Semitic language similar to Hebrew which was the home language of Palestinian Jews of Jesus' day.

Greek *christos* because they are transliterated, *not* translated.

It could be argued that this similarity is because Spanish and English have a common historic influence from Latin, and that the word *Christ* came into each language via the Latin. As we will see, there is a strong element of truth in this, but this commonality has only served to confuse, rather than clarify the meaning.

Just for the sake of argument, look at two non-Latin language Bibles. The first is from the African Swahili language translation, done by the International Bible Society[6]

> 38. Yesu akageuka akawaona wakimfuata akawauliza, "Mnataka nini?" Wakamwambia, ' '**Rabi**' . . . 41. Mara baada ya haya Andrea alikwenda kumtafuta ndugu yake akamwambia, "Tumemwona **Masihi**," yaani **Kristo**.

Next, travel east to the Philippines, where Tagalog is the most common language.[7]

> 38. Paglingon ni Jesus at nakita silang sumusunod. Sinabi niya sa kanila: Ano ang nyong hinahanap? Sinabi nila sa kaniya: **Rabbi**, na kung liliwanagin ay Guro, saan ka nakatira? . . . 41. Una niyang hinanap ang kaniyang sariling kapatid na si Simon at sinabi sa kaniya: Natagpuan namin ang Mesiyas. Ang kahulugan ng **Mesiyas** ay **Cristo**.

6 This IBS translation of the New Testament is for the Tanzanian dialect of the Swahili language, which is primarily used in the United Republic of Tanzania. An estimated 30 million people speak this language as their mother tongue. This translation uses an informal language style and applies a meaning-based translation philosophy. It was translated consulting the biblical languages and was completed in 1989.

7 Tagalog is the most spoken Philippine language in terms of number of speakers. The selection is from Ang Salita ng Diyos translation.

I have again taken the liberty of emphasizing the words under consideration. Note that in these cases, since we have no knowledge of Swahili or Tagalog, we cannot even identify which word represents teacher in those languages, but we have no problem finding the match for the words which have been transliterated from the Greek text, such as *Christo*! There is no doubt that an appeal to common Latin roots cannot be made in these examples, and we must acknowledge that the Greek word *christos* is simply not being translated beyond the Greek. Ultimately, that also means that no real, end-language meaning is being imparted to the reader by its use. (Again, it is important that we remember the distinction between translation and transliteration: *translation conveys meaning; transliteration conveys sound.*)

ANCIENT WORDS FROM LONG-DEAD TONGUES

So why did John include both the original Aramaic and the translated Greek terms in the first place?

John opened both his gospel and his first letter similarly— with philosophic claims well understood by the Greek and Jewish readers of his day.[8] But he does not remain merely philosophical; instead, he jolts his readers by claiming that the Platonic and Gnostic ideal of pure, untouchable, spiritual truth (the *Logos* or *Word*, which under-girded and created

---

8 Gary M. Burge in *Basics of biblical Greek Grammar 2ⁿᵈ Ed.* by William D. Mounce (Zondervan , Grand Rapids, Michigan, 2003), p. 75.

physical reality but could not touch or be touched by it) had invaded history in person, in the form of Jesus of Nazareth! "In the beginning was the Word, and the Word was with God and the Word was God... And the Word became flesh and dwelt among us, and we saw His glory...." "What was from the beginning, what we have heard, what we have seen with our own eyes, what we have looked at and touched with our hands concerning the Word of Life..."

These statements were a bold claim on John's part—a startling contention that he was not simply presenting a new philosophy or a reformed Jewish sect, but the fulfillment of the deepest desire of the Greek and Jewish psyche—the desire to know truth. In Jesus, truth was no longer a hidden shadow in a cave, or an untouchable secret knowledge, but as a real Human who came with power and authority, demonstrating that He had the complete right to be the..., but we are getting ahead of ourselves!

Under the direction of the Holy Spirit, John continues his historical account, moving quickly from broad philosophic claims to the actual story of Jesus' dusty, real-world rural life in first-century Palestine. While his subject is clearly epic, he does not choose to use the poetic style of the classic Greeks; instead John writes as the simple fisherman he is, using the common Greek of his day. He puts his readers right in the middle of the action by making frequent use of the Greek historical present. (This is indicated by the numerous stars found in the *New American Standard Bible* version of his Gospel.)[9]

Additionally, he keeps his readers in the action of the story by allowing them to hear the actual sounds of speakers recorded in his dialogs. Because of this, we have the four word pairs that we've been considering.

Using these techniques, John is emphasizing the fact that his story is real, a historical account of something that actually occurred in time and space. There is nothing akin to this in the epic poems of classical Greece. If there were, there might not be such argument over how classical Greek was pronounced,[10] or if the epics were intended to be understood as real history.[11] But John does intend for us to understand him in this way. And so, even today we are privileged to hear echoes of words uttered by real people in long-dead tongues from almost 2,000 years ago—words such as *rabbi*, *messiah* and *Cephas*.

These words are Aramaic, however, and John was writing to

---

9 The introduction to the NASB states: "A star is used to mark verbs that are historical presents in the Greek which have been translated with an English past tense in order to conform to modern usage. The translators recognized that in some contexts the present tense seems more unexpected and unjustified to the English reader than a past tense would have been. But Greek authors frequently used the present tense for the sake of heightened vividness, thereby transporting their readers in imagination to the actual scene at the time of occurrence. However, the translators felt that it would be wise to change these historical presents to English past tenses."

10 W. J. Purton, *Pronunciation of Ancient Greek* (BiblioLife LLC, 2008).

11 Moses I. Finley and Simon Hornblower, *The World of Odysseus* (London, England: Folio Society, 2002).

a Greek-speaking audience. Though many of his readers were Jews, most of them were more comfortable with Greek than they were with Hebrew,[12] and many of them from areas outside of the immediate middle east would not have been comfortable with Aramaic.

This fact can most-easily be appreciated when we consider the context of the miracle of tongues that occurred at the celebration of Pentecost, as recorded in Acts chapter two. All those visitors to Jerusalem, hearing the good news of Jesus in their own languages, were Jews by birth or proselytes! In addition, the most widely read version of the Old Testament was not Hebrew, but rather the Greek Septuagint, and it was this version that was quoted almost exclusively by both Jesus and His followers.[13]

Because of this, John not only provided the sounds of the Aramaic words, but also provided the Greek translation of them. He let his readers hear the Aramaic *rabbi* by using the Greek characters ραββι (*rabbi*), and then provided the Greek word Διδάσκαλε, (*Didaskale*) as a translation. He then did the same for the Aramaic *messiah,* using the Greek letters Μεσσίαν, (*Messian*), then translating it to the Greek word χριστός, (*christos*). Today it is left for us to discover what

---

12 Nigel Turner, *Grammatical Insights Into the New Testament* (New York: Continuum International Publishing Group, 2004), 180. Turner goes so far to say that based on an analysis of the New Testament texts; "From this evidence one would suppose that Jesus knew the scriptures in Greek but not in Hebrew."

13 Ibid.

English word we should use in translating this Greek word *christos*, as well as its Aramaic original, *messiah*.

First, though, it would be prudent to consider how others have answered the *christos* question.

The simplest answer should be to check a dictionary, and all give basically the same definition. I happen to have a *Webster's New World Dictionary with Student Handbook*[14] in front of me, and it states: Christ (krīst) [< LL. < Gr. christos, the anointed (in NT. Messiah) < chriein, to anoint] Jesus of Nazareth, regarded by Christians as the Messiah prophesied in the Old Testament.

There you have it, short and sweet, without any mystery or intrigue. The English word *Christ* is taken from the Greek word *christos,* which means "the anointed" and is equivalent to the Aramaic word Messiah. Case closed—or is it?

The fact of the matter is that virtually no one thinks *anointed* when they hear the word Christ, nor do any popular translations of the Bible use it as a translation of the Greek *christos*.

The issue is clouded further by the fact that more and more English translations are following the trend, as seen in the *Today's New International Version (TNIV)*,[15] of irregularly rendering the Greek word *christos* into English as *Messiah*—an

---

14 No Author Identified, *Webster's New World Dictionary with Student Handbook : Young People's Edition* (Southwestern, 1978).

15 Ronald F. Youngblood, *Zondervan TNIV Study Bible.* (Zondervan, 2006).

Aramaic word.[16] The translators must believe that the average English-speaking reader is more familiar with the meaning of the Aramaic word *messiah* than were the Jews of John's day.

This growing use of *messiah* in place of *christos* by translators seems to also be driven by a recognition that *christos* is not a name. *Messiah* has the advantage of being a title, but it has been subject to the same obfuscation as *christos*. English dictionaries say it means "promised one" or "deliverer," which misses the Aramaic or Hebrew equivalent entirely.

In short, they are still transliterating rather than translating!

And do remember, John is the only New Testament author to use the word *messiah*. He does so twice,[17] and both times he also provides the translation as *christos* in the immediate context.

It should also be noted that besides conveying sound, as is appropriate in the case of proper nouns, transliteration has at least two other legitimate uses—it may be used when the true meaning of the word being translated is unknown, or when there is no equivalent word in the target language. As we will see, neither of these cases applies here.

In order to understand why *messiah* or *christos* should not normally be translated using the word *anointed*, it is

---

16 Many assume this to be a Hebrew word, and while it is similar to the Hebrew mashiach, it is not the same.

17 John 1:41,4:25

important to remember the distinction between denotation and connotation. The denotation of a word is where it comes from—its origin. In the dictionary definition for *Christ,* above, the denotation is given in brackets as "the anointed." *Anointed* means, literally, "smeared with oil."

On the other hand, the connotation is what people think and feel when they use the word; what we typically call the definition. Usually the denotation and connotation are the same, or at least very close. Sometimes, however, the two can be quite different, as in the following somewhat humorous example.

Consider the English word *nice* and its Spanish cognate, *necia.* Few English speakers would consider it an insult to be described as nice, but any dictionary will tell you that its denotation is from the Latin *nescius,* which means ignorant. *Nice* is generally translated into Spanish with *amable*, which translates back into English as amiable, or friendly, so it is not really equivalent. The Spanish word *necia* literally means fool, and has retained more of the meaning of the original Latin than has English. In a related but opposite manner, the equivalent of the English speaker's "April Fool's Day" is the Latino *Dia de Inocentes.* The English *innocent* retains more of the original Latin significance of "not wicked" than does the Spanish *inocente,* which places more emphasis on the aspect of ignorance.

All of this is to say that, while the denotation of a word may be interesting and helpful in understanding the relationship between words, it would be dangerous to assume that the connotation is always equivalent to it. After all, if a husband called his wife a very nice lady, she would not be justified in replying "How dare you call me ignorant!" In the same way, to translate *christos* as anointed is not necessarily justified unless Greek speakers literally thought "smeared with oil" when they used the term.

AND THE ANSWER IS...

Which finally brings us to the question, "What *did* Greek speakers think when they used or heard the word *christos*?" Again, the denotation of the word is "to smear or rub with oil or grease," which is virtually parallel to the denotation of the Aramaic word *messiah*, or the English word *anointed*.

But did the Greeks actually think of "someone smeared with oil" when they heard *christos*?

The answer to this question can be found by investigating the context in which the word is used. There is no better place to start than the passage that started our quandary in the first place—John chapter one. You will recall that Philip and Andrew, both former disciples of John the Baptizer, had accepted Jesus' call to follow Him. Andrew promptly went and told his brother about Jesus, introducing Him as "the

Messiah." This title, John assures us, means *christos* in the Greek.

Philip, on the other hand, goes to Nathanael and tells him, in verse 45: "We have found Him of whom Moses in the Law and also the Prophets wrote—Jesus of Nazareth, the son of Joseph." Clearly, Andrew is using other words to say the same thing that Philip did; Moses and the prophets wrote of the Messiah. Unlike John, Nathanial is less than convinced, apparently familiar with Nazareth and its denizens, he responds, "Can any good thing come out of Nazareth?" Philip pragmatically tells him, "Come and see."

What follows is more interesting for what it does not say than for what it does. Before Nathanael even has a chance to be introduced to Jesus, Jesus salutes him as "an Israelite indeed in whom there is no deceit!" It was an unusual greeting, to say the least. Something strange seems to be going on behind the scenes here, for rather than saying "Thanks," or something similar, Nathanael responds with "How do you know me?" If Jesus were merely being polite or mildly complementary, such a response could be considered arrogant. Kind of like saying, "Yeah, I'm an honest guy; what of it?" Instead, it seems that Jesus is referring to some particular event, rather than to Nathanael's general character, and Nathanael's suspicious reply reinforces this view, as does what follows. Jesus says, "Before Philip called you, when you were under the fig tree,

I saw you." And here Nathanael's response seems completely over the top and out of context—"Teacher, You are the Son of God; You are the King of Israel!"

I remember seeing a comic book version of this story as a child in Sunday school. It showed Nathanael idyllically lounging under a tree, only to be interrupted by Philip breathlessly running up to him to tell him about Jesus. The problem with this picture is that it misses the point. Clearly, Nathanael is not simply amazed that Jesus has a sort of supernatural telescopic vision and knew his location. He is shocked because Jesus' answer reveals that He truly *knows* him. While we may never know what really happened to Nathanael under the fig tree, it seems clear that something monumental occurred in his life under the fig tree—something that Nathanael fully believed was secret.

While it is pure conjecture, I like to think that Nathanael had had an opportunity to participate in some scheme for personal or political profit that required deception on his part, and that after much internal debate he finally settled the issue under the fig tree. Or perhaps the fig tree was where he met his potential co-conspirators and informed them of his decision not to participate. Whatever it was, it is clear that Nathanael was shocked at Jesus' knowledge—and at Jesus' commendation of him. Clearly, Jesus Himself realized the profound impact of His revelation to Nathanael, because when He promised Nathanael that he would see even greater things than this, He did not mention any of the great miracles of His earthly ministry, nor even His own resurrection, but an event so great that we are all still waiting for it.

Regardless of how you feel about the above interpretation of Nathanael's call and the reason for his explosive confession, it is the actual content of his confession that concerns us here. Nathanael's confession demonstrates his complete reversal from absolute skepticism to absolute acceptance of Philip's claim to have found the One foretold by Moses and the prophets—the *christos*. And what a confession it is: "Teacher, You are the Son of God; You are the King of Israel!"

Obviously, when Nathanael thought of the messiah or *christos,* he thought of a king. So, here in John chapter one (the same chapter that first revealed our lack of understanding of the meaning of the word *christos*) we find our first hint of the real-life meaning of that word.

It is only a hint, however, because Nathanael seems to make two different statements in his confession—"You are the Son of God; You are the King of Israel!" At this point, we are not prepared to say if he viewed one or the other, or both phrases as being equivalent to *christos*, or if he thought of them as mere attributes or descriptors of Him. So while we are closer to our answer, we must continue our search.

We need to look a little closer at Nathanael's wonderful

confession and its two distinct statements. Is Nathanael confessing that Jesus is two different things—both the Son of God and the King of Israel—or is he simply repeating the same thought and restating it in different words?

For those of us blessed (or crippled) by 2,000 years of theological hindsight, the answer appears obvious: Of course he was making two statements. We know that Jesus is both the Son of God and the King of Israel. Only a heretic or infidel would question these truths.... Again, I ask your indulgence to hear me out. I am not questioning the truth of Jesus' divine sonship, but I am questioning if it is sound hermeneutics to consider Nathanael's confession in John chapter one as substantiating it. Far from being a detour, our consideration of this question will lead us directly to the solution of our original puzzle; just what does *christos* mean?

In Romans 1:1–4, Paul begins one of the most profound theological treatises ever written with what, on close examination, appear to be some rather disturbing words:

> Paul, a servant of Christ Jesus, called to be an apostle and set apart for the gospel of God—the gospel he promised beforehand through his prophets in the Holy Scriptures regarding his Son, who as to his earthly life was a descendant of David, and who through the Spirit of holiness was appointed the Son of God in power by his resurrection from the dead: Jesus Christ our Lord. (NIV)

It almost sounds like Paul is saying that Jesus became the Son of God. In fact, as much as it might disturb us, that is exactly what he is saying. A thoughtful person will say "But wait just a minute, before you get to verse four, verse three already describes Him as God's Son, so how can the Son of God become the Son of God? An excellent question, and I cannot answer it better than Thomas Schreiner does in a devotional included in "Basics of biblical Greek Grammar," billed as the most popular first year Greek text used today.

> The two stages of salvation history are present here. During his earthly life Jesus was the Messiah and the Son of David, but upon his resurrection he was appointed as the ruling and reigning Messiah. The title "Son of God" in verse 4, then, refers to the messianic Kingship of Jesus, not his deity. Paul is not suggesting that Jesus was adopted as God's Son upon his resurrection.... The "Son" was appointed by God to be "the Son of God." In other words, Jesus was already the Son before he was appointed to be the Son of God! The first usage (v.3) of the word "Son," then, refers to Jesus' pre-existent divinity that he shared with the Father from all eternity. Jesus' appointment as "the Son of God" (v.4) refers to his installment as the messianic King at his resurrection.[18]

---

18 William D. Mounce, *Basics of biblical Greek Grammar*, 2nd ed. (Zondervan, 2003), 270.

Put simply, Schreiner is stating the well-attested fact that "Son of God" is an ancient idiom[19] for divinely appointed ruler.[20] (A thoughtful reader armed with this understanding should not have a difficult time finding other examples of this usage in the New Testament.) With the above understanding, Nathanael's confession suddenly comes into sharp focus. Nathanael is not making two unrelated statements, the first of which would be strangely anachronistic, given that Philip had just introduced Jesus to him as the "son of Joseph." Rather, he speaks as a typical Judean of his day, using Greek words to express his Hebrew mindset, to the extent that we can see in his emotional outburst the hallmark of Hebrew poetry—parallelism. "You are the Son of God; You are the King of Israel." These are not two statements, but one hymn acknowledging the truth that Andrew and Philip had already realized: Here was the one foretold by Moses and the prophets; the Son of God, the Messiah, the *Christos*—which, being interpreted into English is . . . the KING!

---

19 Donald Juel, *Messianic Exegesis* (Augsburg Fortress Publishers, 1998), 80. "The early character of the association between king and sonship is established by the confessional fragment to which Paul makes reference.... The reference to being "designated" to sonship indicates that it is conceived as an office into which one is installed. The royal character of the office is established by the reference to descent from David. There is no contradiction between being descended "from [the seed of] David according to the flesh" and "designated Son of God."

20 Specifically he says "messianic King" but as we see, this is a grammatically unwarranted redundancy that reveals a lack of understanding of the word messiah.

TWO

THE CASE FOR KING IN THE OLD TESTAMENT

"For the first time in all those years she tasted the word King itself with all linked associations of battle, marriage, priesthood, mercy, and power." —C. S. LEWIS, *THAT HIDEOUS STRENGTH*

Christos means king!

Again, this is not necessarily a new truth, but it is a glorious one indeed!

That Jesus is King is something that has been readily attested to by his followers throughout the ages, and yet there is a sense in which the revelation is unexpected and disconcerting. If *christos* really does mean king, why hasn't it been translated that way, and why aren't people aware of this issue? Why weren't you aware of it?

A SUCKER EVERY MINUTE?

I have found that when I first share these thoughts with people, there is almost always an immediate and joyous acceptance of the idea that *christos* should be translated as king, not to mention an incredulity that the word has been used so glibly and without comprehension.

Soon, however, many of these same people become concerned that they are being suckered. "After all, who does this guy think he is to say that all the pastors and teachers I ever had have missed something so simple? Isn't it more likely that this new idea is ill-founded? Why should I believe that all the Bibles we have ever seen, and all the churches we have ever attended got this wrong?"

Perhaps it is premature to jump to this conclusion.... After all, is it really legitimate to try to overturn millennia of familiar word usage based on consideration of just a few biblical texts?

If this is your reaction, I have no criticism for you, as I've been there myself. Certainly, we must be careful not to be tossed about by every wind of doctrine—or of vocabulary. But, having concluded the previous chapter by (finally!) revealing that I believe the Greek word *christos* and the Aramaic word *messiah* are best represented by the English word *king*, please come with me to examine if this thesis can hold up to closer scrutiny and the test of broader biblical use. After that, it will be time to ask if it even matters.

First, however, we need to return to the issue of the academically preferred meaning of *christos,* which, you will recall from our previous conversation, is "anointed."

Meanwhile, it is important to note that almost every cult that has had any measure of success has succeeded by exploiting some truth or practice that was erroneously underemphasized or was absent from the church. At the same time, it is also sad to point out that many of the current intellectual attacks on scripture are only effective because many church leaders have tried to protect their flocks from exposure to supposedly difficult ideas, or challenges to what they consider normative Christian beliefs.

For example, Bart D. Ehrman[21] is upsetting the faith of some—and confirming the agnosticism of many—by "revealing" certain spurious passages in scripture, such as John 7:53–8:11, a passage so well known that scholars generally refer to it by its name, "*Pericope Adulterae,*" rather than by its scriptural reference. Conservative Bible scholars have long been virtually unanimous in acknowledging that this passage is not part of the original Gospel but a later addition. In spite of their knowledge of this, many pastors choose not to inform their charges of this fact, unreasonably fearing that this might weaken their flock's view of scripture. Even

---

21 Bart D. Ehrman, *Misquoting Jesus: The Story Behind Who Changed the Bible & Why* (New York: HarperCollins, 2005).

worse, many still choose to use known spurious passages in their preaching and teaching, rather than doing the harder work of teaching the often legitimate truths found in these passages from more obscure but *bona fide* texts.

Wouldn't it be better to trust the laity with the truth and a basic knowledge of textual criticism, so that they can have a ready answer to infidels[22] such as Dr. Ehrman?[23] The truth is that our ability to separate the wheat from the chaff of ancient texts is an essential evidence that we can indeed trust scripture. Conservative biblical scholarship has not eliminated all uncertainty from the biblical texts, but it has certainly reduced it to such a point that we can have great confidence that what we read when we open our Bibles is trustworthy.

In a similar vein, is it possible that *Christ* and *Messiah* really do mean "anointed," and we are only susceptible to this new kingly interpretation because the intellectual leadership of the church has tried to protect us from confusion, or because they think it is an unimportant distinction? On the surface, this argument seems plausible. After all, a high percentage of pastors and educated laypeople, when asked, respond that Christ means anointed, and, as noted in the previous

---

22 Dr. Ehrman is more accurately characterized as an apostate, since he started his career as an evangelical. He himself is an example of the dangers of saving these types of revelations until graduate school or seminary.

23 "Bible.org: The Gospel according to Bart," http://www.bible.org/page.php?page_id=4000. An excellent defense of this position and rebuttal of Dr. Ehrman's work.

chapter, this is what the dictionary seems to say. Since there is no disagreement that *christos* is the Greek equivalent of the Hebrew word *mashiach*, (which is often confused with the Aramaic *messiah*) perhaps we should take another step back, and look at *mashiach* a little closer.

The King Foreshadowed

When we look at the Hebrew there are actually two Hebrew words which we should consider: *mashiach*, a noun originally meaning "the anointed one or thing," and *mashach*, a verb which meant "to anoint." The English word "anoint," you will recall, means "to smear or rub with oil or grease."

We have already spoken of the distinction between *connotation* and *denotation* and understand that, ultimately, it is the *usage* of a word that determines its meaning. Clearly, "Jesus, the one smeared with oil," doesn't ring any emotional bells when contrasted with "Jesus Christ,"[24] so we must ask ourselves, "How did this usage develop?"

These two Hebrew words are used about 110 times in the Old Testament, but a closer examination reveals that there is a distinct division between their usage in the Pentateuch and how they are used in the rest of the Hebrew scriptures.

In the books of Moses, these words are found approximately 30 times. Each time they are used in reference to the

---

24 This alone is sufficient to explain why few translations have rendered *christos* as anointed.

consecration of things or people set apart for ceremonial religious use. A representative example of each follows.

> Moses then took the anointing oil and anointed [*mashach*] the tabernacle and all that was in it, and consecrated them. He sprinkled some of it on the altar seven times and anointed [*mashach*] the altar and all its utensils, and the basin and its stand, to consecrate them. Then he poured some of the anointing oil on Aaron's head and anointed [*mashach*] him, to consecrate him. (Leviticus 8:8-12) Then the anointed [*mashiach*] priest is to take some of the blood of the bull and bring it to the tent of meeting. (Leviticus 4:5)

In each of these examples it can be clearly seen that the English *anointed* could just as well be replaced with *consecrated*, as either a verb or a noun, with no loss of understanding. If this pattern holds (and you can easily confirm that it does) we are safe in saying that the connotation of *anoint* and *anointed* in the Pentateuch is: "to consecrate or set apart for ceremonial use, or the person or object so consecrated." The actual act of smearing with oil was the visible, physical means of signifying the consecration.

Interestingly, this use of *anointed* is certainly in keeping with many people's conception of the Christ, and is in absolute conformity with the teaching of Hebrews that Jesus is our High Priest. With that in mind, perhaps, in addition to "king" we should add "consecrated one" to our understanding of the meaning of *christos*.

This understanding of *mashach* is well and good for Genesis through Deuteronomy, but what do we find in the rest of the Old Testament?

Evidently, in the 200 or more years between the end of Moses' life and the time of Gideon's sons, the word *anointed* underwent a subtle but significant change. The word still retained the original significance of "sanctification" or "appointment for a special purpose," but that purpose has a far more specific, focused usage.

Gideon's son, Jotham, gives us our first post-Mosaic use of the term. When Jotham's brother, who had just been declared the ruler of Shechem, killed his other 68 brothers in an attempt to guarantee the security of his position, Jotham directed a parable against him. He says:

> "Listen to me, O men of Shechem, that God may listen to you. Once the trees went forth to anoint [*mashach*] a king over them, and they said to the olive tree, 'Reign over us!' But the olive tree said to them, 'Shall I leave my fatness with which God and men are honored, and go to wave over the trees?' Then the trees said to the fig tree, 'You come, reign over us!' But the fig tree said to them, 'Shall I leave my sweetness and my good fruit, and go to wave over the trees?' Then the trees said to the vine, 'You come, reign over us!' But the vine said to them, 'Shall I leave my new wine, which cheers God and men, and go to wave over the trees?' Finally all the trees said to the bramble, 'You come, reign over us!' The bramble said to the trees, 'If in truth you are anointing [*mashach*] me as king over

you, come and take refuge in my shade; but if not, may
fire come out from the bramble and consume the cedars
of Lebanon." (Judges 9:7-15)

Jotham's parable uses "anointing" in a context familiar to all who have more than a passing acquaintance with the Old Testament—in reference to the installation of a king. While this is the first biblical occasion where *mashach* is used in this way, it is far from the last. In fact, throughout the rest of the Old Testament, *mashach* is used almost exclusively in this way—with reference to a king.

A typical example of both the verb and noun form being used together in the same context, is in the popular Bible story of Samuel's discovery of God's choice of David as the King of Israel. God tells Samuel:

> "You shall invite Jesse to the sacrifice, and I will show you what you shall do; and you shall anoint [*mashach*] for Me the one whom I designate to you." So Samuel did what the LORD said, and came to Bethlehem. And the elders of the city came trembling to meet him and said, "Do you come in peace?" He said, "In peace; I have come to sacrifice to the LORD. Consecrate yourselves and come with me to the sacrifice." He also consecrated Jesse and his sons and invited them to the sacrifice. When they entered, he looked at Eliab and thought, "Surely the LORD'S anointed [*mashiach*] is before Him." But the LORD said to Samuel, "Do not look at his appearance or at the height of his stature, because I have rejected him; for God sees not as man sees, for man looks at the outward appearance, but the LORD looks at the heart." (I Samuel 16:3-7)

The story continues, of course, with Samuel passing over the first seven sons of Jesse, only to find that none of them was God's choice. It is not until David, the youngest son, is summoned in from tending his father's sheep, that the true anointed, or king, is found.

And so it continues across the Old Testament, with the verb being used to signify the appointment of a king, and the noun being used as an idiom for the king himself. It is also interesting to note that, in this passage, ceremonial consecration is no longer strictly associated with the act of anointing. Instead, the act of ceremonial consecration seems to shift toward ceremonial washings, a practice continued in the church today in the form of baptism.[25]

In Psalm two, the first of the aptly (yet for most, unintelligibly) named "Messianic Psalms," we find a particularly revealing case of the use of the word *anointed*.

First, though, keep in mind that one of the often-noted blessings of Hebrew poetry is that its word play does not depend primarily on rhyme or meter as English and Greek poetry does, nor on syllabification as the Japanese Haiku does. This is not to say that these entities are never present, only that they are secondary.

Instead, Hebrew poetics are expressed through various intricate patterns, including parallelism and chiasm. As a

---

25 1 Peter 3:21

result, Hebrew poetry, unlike the other languages mentioned, can be largely appreciated in any language without any knowledge of Hebrew itself. In contrast, I can testify from personal experience that the lyrics of popular songs in Spanish or English often bear little resemblance to their translated counterparts and are only identifiable due to common melodies. Not so with the Psalms! Psalm 23 makes just as beautiful and meaningful a wall plaque in English as it does in Spanish—thanks to the fundamental nature of Hebrew poetry.

Now let us look at the psalm in question.

Psalm 2: The Reign of the LORD's Anointed.

1. *Why are the nations in an uproar*
   And the peoples devising a vain thing?
2. *The kings of the earth take their stand*
   And the rulers take counsel together
   Against the LORD and against His Anointed, saying,
3. *"Let us tear their fetters apart*
   And cast away their cords from us!"
4. *He who sits in the heavens laughs,*
   The Lord scoffs at them.
5. *Then He will speak to them in His anger*
   And terrify them in His fury, saying,
6. *"But as for Me, I have installed My King*
   Upon Zion, My holy mountain."
7. *"I will surely tell of the decree of the LORD:*
   He said to Me, 'You are My Son,
   Today I have begotten You.
8. *'Ask of Me, and I will surely give the*
   nations as Your inheritance, And the very
   ends of the earth as Your possession.

9. *'You shall break them with a rod of iron,*
   You shall shatter them like earthenware.'"
10. *Now therefore, O kings, show discernment;*
    Take warning, O judges of the earth.
11. *Worship the LORD with reverence*
    And rejoice with trembling.
12. *Do homage to the Son, that He not become angry,*
    and you perish in the way, For His wrath may soon be
    kindled How blessed are all who take refuge in Him!

Can there be any question that "His Anointed" in verse two is exactly he same one as "My King" in verse six? Would we lose anything if we retitled the psalm *"The Reign of the Lord's King?"* Of course not!

In fact, it is David's experience and subsequent use of the term that seems to solidify the use of *anointed* as a cognate for *king* in the rest of the Old Testament.

It is legitimate to ask what David was thinking as he wrote this psalm. Do you think he looked at it after he composed it and thought "Wow, that's weird. I wonder where that came from?" This is as unlikely as the question is facetious; in reality David knew that he was the Lord's anointed, or king,[26] and he very explicitly states this in the last verse of Psalm 18:

> He gives great deliverance to His king, And shows loving kindness to His anointed, To David and his descendants forever. (Psalm 18:50)

26 This in no way reduces the truth or impact of the fact that this Psalm also refers to Jesus of Nazareth, only that it seems unlikely that David was aware of this significance when he wrote it.

Here again, the parallelism of Hebrew poetry makes it clear that the words *king* and *anointed* are absolutely synonymous.

So, even with this in mind, you may still be surprised to discover that the Old Testament teaches that David was the christ. But that is exactly what he was called in the Septuagint—the Greek Bible that Jesus and His ambassadors used. The fact that this comes as a surprise in and of itself indicates that translators have indeed obscured rather than revealed the significance of *christos*.

Even more troubling in Psalm two is verse seven, and—unless you remember our discussion in chapter one of Paul's opening to his letter to the assembly in Rome—you may well think that David is guilty of blasphemy. The fact is that David recognized that he had become the "son of God" on the same day that God had declared him king—a fact that actually applies to us as well.

I realize that this understanding is difficult for some evangelicals to accept, but I urge you to remember the warning found earlier in this chapter. When we shy away from seemingly difficult biblical passages or concepts, we provide our enemy with an opportunity. And we certainly understand that the enemy will use any opportunity he can to plant doubt concerning the Word of God; inevitably, one of his most potent tools is our own ignorance.

Theological liberals tout the fact that David saw himself as the messiah and the son of God, as if it somehow diminishes the claims of Jesus of Nazareth, and conservatives seem to ignore the issue as if it were somehow a legitimate argument. We should be able to recognize that David was the *christos*, the king and savior of God's people, and at the same time recognize that this was a feeble foreshadowing of the glories to be revealed in Jesus, our true king. Quite simply, if we are not offended at the Passover lambs, we should not be disturbed by the Old Testament christs.

The use of the word *anointed*, of course, does not end with David; it is found throughout the rest of the Old Testament. Of the almost 100 times that *mashiach* and *mashach* are used in scripture after the Pentateuch, there is only one case in which it is clearly not used in a royal association. In Isaiah, we find:

> They set the table, they spread out the cloth, they eat, they drink; "Rise up, captains, oil [*mashach*] the shields," (Isaiah 21:5)

Presumably, in this usage the shields were made of leather and were given the same treatment a present-day baseball player gives his glove. A more interesting case of the use of the word *mashach* is found in Jeremiah 22:14, where this word is used in an extremely uncharacteristic way; so much so, in fact, that it is the only case in which it is not translated as some form of the English word "anoint," and has no apparent connection with oil or grease. The *Young's Concordance* I was using gave the word as "paint," and so I thought there were two clear exceptions, until I looked up the verse and read it in the context seen below (emphasis added):

> For thus says the LORD in regard to Shallum the son of Josiah, king of Judah, who became king in the place of Josiah his father, who went forth from this place,

> "He will never return there;
> but in the place where they led him captive,
> there he will die and not see this land again.
> **Messages about the Kings**
> Woe to him who builds his house without righteousness
> and his upper rooms without justice, who
> uses his neighbor's services without pay
> and does not give him his wages,
> who says, *'I will build myself a roomy house
> with spacious upper rooms, and
> cut out its windows,
> paneling it with cedar and painting
> [mashach] it bright red. Do you become a
> king because you are competing in cedar?*
> Did not your father eat and drink and
> do justice and righteousness?
> Then it was well with him.
> He pled the cause of the afflicted and needy;
> Then it was well.
> Is not that what it means to know Me?[27]"
> Declares the LORD. "But your eyes and
> your heart are intent only upon your own

---

27 It is not germane to our topic, but I feel compelled to point out how different this is from the popular Christian idea of what it means to know God.

dishonest gain, and on shedding innocent blood
and on practicing oppression and extortion."
Jeremiah 22:11-17

Now, instead of being an exception, this particular usage becomes one of the stronger pieces of evidence that we are on the right track.[28] Simply considering the emphasized portion above, we can now understand Jeremiah's seemingly out-of-place use of the word. He is making an elegant pun that would have been instantly caught by his readers, but is revealed to us only if we understand the connotation, as opposed to the denotation, of the word *mashach*. Here the use of the word is so far removed from its denotation that an entirely new and unique English word is required for its translation. Jeremiah's use of this word makes no sense, unless its use in relation to king-making is understood. For Jeremiah, *mashach* meant "king-making," and its denotation of "rubbed with oil or grease" had faded into such obscurity that he could equate it with painting a room in a house.[29]

To summarize, then, we can see that the connotation, or meaning, of the verb *mashach* in the Old Testament, except for in the Pentateuch, is "to make king." Isaiah 21:5 becomes

28 One of the great joys of scientific discovery and evidence of correctness of a new idea is that it gives back more than is put into it. Sadi Carnot's study of heat led to the formulation of the laws of thermodynamics, which informed Ludwig Boltzmann's study of the behavior of gases, which led ultimately to Claude Shannon's discovery of the laws governing information transfer, which today continues giving new insights in the area of quantum physics.

29 It is also possible that rubbing the cedar with oil preserved it like paint and brought out its red color, but the pun still is clear.

the lone exception which proves the rule, and Jeremiah 22:12 becomes the paradigm of Hebraic thought. From the book of Judges on, the noun *mashiach*, often equated with the Aramaic *messias*, and translated in the Septuagint as *christos*, is without exception synonymous with the English word "king."

Three

THE CASE FOR
KING IN THE
NEW TESTAMENT

"...for as there are certain names common to kings, as Arsaces among the Persians, Caesar among the Romans, Pharaoh among the Egyptians, so among the Jews a king is called Christos."
—THE RECOGNITIONS OF CLEMENT, CA. 225 AD

"Now unto the king eternal, immortal, invisible, the only wise God, be honour and glory for ever and ever. Amen."
—I TIMOTHY 1:17

BDAG GUMMIT!

Until now, we've essentially relied on the scriptures and the dictionary to define *christos*. However, an English dictionary is not a source that many Greek scholars would consider relevant to the question at hand.

Instead, they would refer you to the impressive-sounding tome, *A Greek-English Lexicon of the New Testament and Other Early Christian Literature*,[30] affectionately known as,

---

30 Walter Bauer, *A Greek-English Lexicon of the New Testament and Other Early Christian Literature*, 1st ed. (University Of Chicago Press, 2001).

and hereafter referred to as, BDAG.[31] Any scholars reading this have, no doubt, long since fetched their copy and are either smugly smirking at my ignorance, or, if they have already read the entry, may be slightly puzzled by what they found in their big red book.

BDAG gives two renderings for Χριστός, and the first is what we have come to expect: "(1) fulfiller of Israelite expectation of a deliverer, the Anointed One, the Messiah, the Christ..." The second rendition should cause evangelicals, at least, to question what is going on here: "(2) the personal name ascribed to Jesus, Christ, which many gentiles must have understood in this way (to them it seemed very much like Χρηστός...)."

That last word is transliterated as *chrestos*, and BDAG proceeds to give several citations demonstrating its use as a Greek surname from the first century. Interestingly, on the facing page, *chrestos* has its own BDAG listing, and there no mention is made of its use as a surname.

Chrestos is found several places in scripture in its own right. In I Corinthians 15:33 it is commonly translated as *good*, which is not an uncommon surname even in English today. That a positive-sounding adjective such as *good* finds its way into use as a surname is not surprising, and few phone books

---

31 This is not to say that there are not other excellent—and some would say better—tools available, only that one runs the risk of not being taken seriously if they fail to reference it.

are without at least one citation of a King.

However, few people have trouble distinguishing a word's use as an adjective from its use as a proper name, or a name from a title. We would be quite surprised to find that hundreds of years from now people were referring to Elvis King as the founder of an early form of rock and roll. People simply don't confuse Presley's name with his appellation of king of rock and roll. BDAG's claim that the adjective *chrestos,* used as a surname, would somehow transform *christos* from a meaningful title to a virtual last name, is suspect. That *chrestos* exists and is similar to *christos* simply does not justify the idea that such a change occurred.

In fact, that second definition is so shocking that you may need to go back and read it a second time, as I did. I had heard this idea before, but usually from people who would be classified as unchurched.

In retrospect, I should not have been so surprised. It turns out I had made the same mistake that I've been warning others of. Maybe you already caught it.

In the initial dictionary definition of Christ given in chapter one, I concentrated on the denotation that was given to such an extent that I completely overlooked the definition that was given. Go back and look, and you will see that the actual *definition* given—and almost any English dictionary will give the same—is "Jesus of Nazareth!"[32]

Now we also find that the preeminent source for understanding New Testament Greek usage is, in effect, likewise saying that the word *christos* in the New Testament should be understood as Jesus' last name! In other words, to use current English vernacular, we should refer to Jesus as Mr. Christ! In reality, though, BDAG is not quite so simplistic and adds the following statement:

> The transition to sense 2 is marked by certain passages in which Χριστός does not mean the Messiah in general (even when the ref. is to Jesus), but a very definite Messiah, Jesus, who now is called Christ not as a title but as a name.

It should be noted that, however *Jesus Christ* was understood in the New Testament, this usage as a name is precisely the way it is routinely employed in English, Spanish, and other languages around the world today, and the way it has been used for almost 1,700 years. *Jesus Christ* is easily and almost universally understood to be the full name of Jesus, as if no further thought is required.

Even on further thought, though, the answer to the meaning of *Christ* usually assumes some form of embedded secret name meaning—as in, Michael means "who is like God?" While understanding name meanings themselves may add fullness and appreciation to a name, the meaning

32 This is why your spell checker will flag christ with a lower case C as misspelled—it is a name!

itself does not replace the use of the name, and especially not when moving from one language to another. In other words, Jesus means "Ya saves," but Ya saves is not His name! When translating, we rightly transliterate a name from the Greek into whatever language we are targeting, and as a result, it should be similar and recognizable regardless what that language might be.

Following its quoted selection above, BDAG goes on to cite 28 New Testament verses[33] in support of the claim of a "transition" from the original sense of *title* to *name*. If this transition is real, one would expect to find some sense of shifting usage of *christos* across those 28 verses, so that earlier references would have more of a title sense and later ones would move more and more exclusively to merely a name sense. We are quickly disappointed, however, as we find the supplied list is in order of New Testament occurrence, and without any attempt at providing a chronological accounting. Moreover there does not seem to be a single instance in which the title *king* does not seem to make more grammatic and semantic sense in the context.

It is also interesting to note that, of the 28 occurrences of *christos* in this list,[34] all but one of them is preceded by the Greek equivalent of *the*, and yet, in only one instance is *the*

---

33 A full listing of these citations can be found in the Appendix.
34 Acts 9:20 does not contain *christos*, and I Cor. 10:16 has it twice.

included in the English translation.

In order to appreciate the significance of this, it is important to understand a little bit about the use of the Greek article *the*.

First, Greek has no equivalent to the English language's indirect articles *a* or *an*. Because of this, it is up to the translator to determine by the context of a passage, and by the demands of English grammar, if a noun should be preceded by an *a* or *an*.

Secondly, the use of the article in Greek does not always coincide with its use in English. That is to say that there are times where Greek might use the article and English would not, and vice versa.

The rule of thumb is that if the Greek text employs the article it should be included in the translation, unless English grammar precludes its use; and that if it is not used in the text, it may be added if English grammar demands it.[35] For example, in English, names are normally accompanied by the direct article only in cases of extreme emphasis, and are often italicized, as in: "You actually spoke with *the* Albert Einstein?" Titles, on the other hand, almost always merit the article when used without the name, as in: On his return *the* President kissed *the* First Lady on the cheek.

---

35 William D. Mounce, *Basics of biblical Greek Grammar*, 2nd ed. (Zondervan, 2003), 38, 39.

Unfortunately, Greek is not nearly so clear cut, and both names and titles are often found with or without an accompanying article. As a result, the consistent use of the article in the above list of 28 verses is not as definitive as we might have hoped.

Still, that does not mean that there is nothing noteworthy here. Remember our rule of thumb: if English allows it, the article should be included in our translation. Remarkably, when we check an English translation (NASB) of the list above, we find that in 27 out of the 28 occurrences of the Greek article associated with the word *christos*, the translators have omitted it from the English!

Please understand, the translators did not choose to render Ο Χριστός as the Anointed, or even as the Christ, both of which would have clearly communicated the original sense of title, but simply as Christ.

If this was a conscious decision, the only explanation that I can conceive for consistently omitting of the article is that—contrary to BDAG's assertion that this list demonstrates a transition in the usage of *christos* from a title to that of a name—the translators themselves truly understood every occurrence of *christos*, except one, to actually be a name. This, after all, is what they are taught from the early days of their very first Greek class. In the very first vocabulary list included in Mounce's popular first year Greek text, he gives Christ as the preferred gloss for *christos*, and then adds this note:

> In the Old Testament and the earlier parts of the New Testament "χριστός" was a title, but as you move through Acts and it becomes so closely associated with Jesus that it becomes a personal name like "Jesus" and should be capitalized (Χριστός).[36]

In fact, I do not actually believe that the translators were thinking of this theoretical transition at all. It is my understanding that these were God-fearing scholars who were doing their best to accurately render the Greek texts into a form readily understood by their English-speaking audience. They were human, however, and we humans are creatures of habit. Therefore, they translated *christos* according to habit.

(While the word habit is often preceded by the word bad, remember that habits are also the Creator's gifts that allow us to multitask and accomplish far more than we could without them. Walking, for example, is an incredibly complex act that requires the coordination of hundreds of muscles responding to literally thousands of sensory inputs. Thanks to habit, we handle this feat on a regular basis, and with virtually no conscious thought.)

In other words, I suspect that the translators, like us, were simply in the habit of hearing and saying "Jesus Christ" and translated the title habitually—as a mere name.

Of course, anyone who has attempted to learn another

---

36 Ibid., 20.

language after the mentally elastic days of childhood can testify to the difficulty of the task. Add to this difficulty the challenge of a full college course load, the fact that everyone tells you how hard that class is, and the fact that the language seems so obscure that the professors can't even agree on how it should be pronounced[37] (let alone converse in it), and you get a sense of what confronts the typical first-year Greek student. Any point of habitual familiarity is latched onto, and cognates quickly become your friends. For that reason, common words and names figure prominently in the early vocabulary lists. Hey, it may be just a list of names, but you are actually reading those weird letters, and it gives you hope that you really can do it. "Any port in a storm," as they say.

It is time that we recognize that *Christ* is an example of one of the great enemies of language acquisition—a false cognate, a treacherous friend that betrays us into complacency by allowing us to think that we understand her meaning, only to expose us to ridicule at the most inopportune moment.

To give a somewhat similar, classic parallel in Spanish, *embarazada* certainly seems to be equivalent to the English word *embarrassed*. If you used it in this sense, however, you would most certainly have cause to be—embarrassed! That

---

37 When I first undertook the task of teaching myself Greek, I was surprised to find that pronunciation was a source of controversy; most teachers use the so-called Erasmun pronunciation which has no relation to either Erasmus, or N.T. Greek. A minority use the Ethnic pronunciation, which is thought to be close to what was used in N.T. Times, but is also thought to be a bit more challenging for beginners, as many vowels and diphthongs have the same sound.

is because the word *embarazada* actually means "pregnant."

Similarly, I well recall the puzzled looks and—later—laughter I received when I tried to explain that the first coat of paint on a building was to be blue. "*El primo es azul,*" I confidently said, forgetting that *primo* meant "cousin," not "first," or "primer." In other words, I was saying "The cousin is blue." I have also had occasion to be directed to the bathroom (*servicio*) when I was asking where the church service (*reunión*) was.

Back to Greek, however, our Χριστός is the third most common regular noun in the New Testament, occurring 529 times. It is exceeded only by "man" (occurring 550 times) and God (1,317 times). Of course, you already understand these words, and they require no further thought to define. Now you must press on to the real work of learning cases, declensions, tenses, voice and aspect.

And so the Greek word Χριστός, that noble title for which the followers of Jesus died, and for which He Himself was crucified, become sublimated under our paltry understanding of the English word *Christ*. Of course, it has a denotation—anointed—but there are few names that don't mean something.

Knowing the denotation becomes one more piece of academic trivia, an easy point on a test. "Now, how am I going to memorize these 18 forms of the Greek word *the* and what the significance of each is by this coming Friday?"

And so it goes, the students eventually become professors who teach more students who...

And ultimately the force of habit goes unchallenged, and the English name *Christ* (it *is* in the dictionary, after all) now becomes the basis for our understanding of the New Testament *christos* it resembles, rather than the other way around.

THE MYSTERY OF THE MISSING KING

As soon as we give credence to the idea that *christos* means king, we also find the solution to another puzzle that we might have easily overlooked.

Think of the countless hymns, popular Christian songs and sermons you have heard which declare "Jesus Christ is King." There are even T-shirts and bumper stickers which boldly proclaim "Jesus Christ is my King," and yet, in reality, this is a strangely unbiblical statement! We simply do not find anything to match the actual construction of these popular phrases in scripture. Nor will you find anything comparable to Schreiner's quote in the first chapter which referred to the "Messianic King" anywhere in the Old Testament.

The reason, quite simply, is that these phrases constitute verbal redundancies, and their usage indicates a lack of understanding of the Aramaic word *messiah* or the Greek *christos*. In short, they amount to saying "King Jesus is King!"

Now if these words did not mean king, as is claimed here, you would expect to find at least one instance of these or similar phrases somewhere in the Bible. Instead, the closest thing we can find in the Old Testament are examples of Hebrew parallelism, similar to those already noted, which only serve to confirm the thesis that *messiah* and *king* truly are different words for the same thought.

In the New Testament, my search to confirm the absence of any statement such a "Jesus Christ is King" led me to Mark 15:31–32, which at first blush certainly seems to be an equivalent statement, at least in English.

> In the same way the chief priests also, along with the scribes, were mocking Him among themselves and saying, "He saved others; He cannot save Himself. Let *this* Christ, the King of Israel, now come down from the cross, so that we may see and believe!" Those who were crucified with Him were also insulting Him. (Mark 15:31–32.)

What I found when I turned to the actual Greek text was astounding. Rather than finding an example that would weaken the argument that *christos* should be translated as king, here was incontrovertible grammatic proof that Greek-speaking Jews of the first century did indeed think that *christos* and *king* were absolutely synonymous.

What follows is easily the most technical part of this book, and I ask your indulgence as it may be tedious. However, even without any previous training in New Testament Greek, you should be able to understand the gist of what follows.

Remember the circumstances that surround this story: a week earlier Jesus had entered Jerusalem to the adulation of her inhabitants in what is commonly called the triumphant entry, an event vividly recalled in John's account of the good news.

> On the next day the large crowd who had come to the feast, when they heard that Jesus was coming to Jerusalem, took the branches of the palm trees and went out to meet Him, and began to shout, "Hosanna! BLESSED IS HE WHO COMES IN THE NAME OF THE LORD, even the King of Israel." Jesus, finding a young donkey, sat on it; as it is written, "FEAR NOT, DAUGHTER OF ZION; BEHOLD, YOUR KING IS COMING, SEATED ON A DONKEY'S COLT." (John 12:12-15)

Since we will deal in more detail with these events in a later chapter, we need only note that Jesus was convicted of treason against Rome. In the passage under consideration, we find Him being executed, by crucifixion, for His crime, with the charge posted over His head. John tells us that the sign read "Jesus the Nazarene, King of the Judeans," and that the charge was posted in three languages. Thus, we find ourselves at the foot of the cross, hearing the chief priests and scribes mocking Him among themselves and saying *"Allous esosen eauton ou dunatai sosai; o Christos o Basileus Israel katabato nun apo tou stavou, ina idomen kai pisteusomen."*

In our passage in Mark 15, we are only interested here in the quote which is split across the two verses: "He saved others; He cannot save Himself. Let this Christ, the King of Israel, come down from the cross that we may see and believe." The first part of the quote contained in verse 31 is straightforward and indisputable; if someone wished to have a translation a little closer to the Greek, it could be rendered as: "Others He saved; Himself He cannot save." However, this would be more awkward English and hence not as good a translation.[38]

Verse 32 begins in English with "Let *this* Christ, the King of Israel, come down ..." The italicized *this* indicates that the word is not found in the original language, but that the translators felt the context implied it. Most likely they were trying to emphasize the incredulity of the speakers, but this does tend more toward interpretation, rather than direct translation.[39] The Greek form of the word translated "come down" is a third person imperative—a form having no English equivalent, but usually indicated by the inclusion of the word *let,* as we find here. What *is* in the Greek text, and yet strangely absent from the English, is, once again, the Greek article *o*, which precedes the word Christ, as can be seen in the transliteration above. I am at a loss to understand why the

---

38 Any who would wish to dispute in absolute terms as to which is a better translation reveals a lack of understanding of the nature of language and the admonition of I Timothy 6:4.

39 A common and sometimes unavoidable problem.

translators did not translate this passage as "Let the Christ, the King of Israel, come down from the cross so that we may see and believe."

Regardless of whether *the* or *this* is included in the translation, there is something going on here which is completely obscure to someone not familiar with Greek. The first four words of verse 32, in Greek, "*o Christos o Basileus*" (ὁ χριστὸς ὁ βασιλεὺς) constitute a construction called a "nominative in simple apposition."[40] Daniel B. Wallace, probably the premier New Testament Greek grammarian of our day, says of this common construction:

> Four features of simple apposition should be noted (the first two are structural clues; the last two are semantic): An appositional construction involves (1) two adjacent substantives (2) in the same case, (3) which refer to the same person or thing, (4) and have the same syntactical relation to the rest of the clause.
> The first substantive can belong to any category (e.g., subject, predicate nom., etc.) and the second is merely a clarification, description, or identification of who or what is mentioned.[41]

Perhaps some examples—English examples—are warranted to clarify the point. This point—the point I am trying to make—needs to be understood. Those who understand—the ones paying attention—will get it. The key thing—the essential

40 An equivalent construction called the "accusative in simple apposition" is used in a similar context in Luke 23:2. The discussion here applies equally to Luke's usage.
41 Ibid.Daniel B. Wallace, *Basics of New Testament Syntax, The*, abridged edition. (Zondervan, 2000), 33.

thing to understand—is that the second noun in the noun pair is "merely a clarification, description, or identification of who or what is mentioned." According to Wallace then, "the King" is "merely a clarification, description, or identification" of *o christos*!

For Greek scholars reading this, any remaining doubt concerning the equivalence of *christos* and *king* should now be removed. Following the model of the English examples just given, and in keeping with our previously noted rule concerning the inclusion of the article, our translation should read, "Let the King, the King of Israel, now come down from the cross so that we may see and believe." One can almost hear the sneer in the voices of the chief priests and scribes as they gloat over the one dying beneath the banner sarcastically declaring His kingship.

A KING BY ANY OTHER NAME

The Greek word for king on the sign on Jesus' cross, however, was not *christos*; it was *basileus* (βασιλεὺς), and it is important to understand why.

We have already learned that Greek was the language of everyday discourse in first-century Palestine. Yet for most of the inhabitants of the area, it was a second language that was learned after Aramaic, which was spoken at home.

That Aramaic was the common language of home and

hearth is indicated in Jesus' desperate cry from the garden of Gethsemane. Mark 14:36 records that He called out *"Abba o Pater,"* or "Daddy Father." *Abba* is not a Hebrew word, but is Aramaic for daddy. In His pain, Jesus called out in the language of His childhood.

Regardless whether Greek or Aramaic was used, the culture was unmistakably Hebrew, and as such, was rooted in the Old Testament. As a result, there is a significant Semitic influence to be found throughout the New Testament.[42]

To understand how this worked, permit me to use yet another example from my experience with Spanish in Costa Rica. *Necesito* is a perfectly good Spanish word meaning "I need," or "I require," and its relation to the English word *necessary* is self-evident. In rural Costa Rica, however, the locals are far more likely to use the word o*cupo*, which, according to my English/Spanish dictionary means "I occupy." I still have not figured this out, but I have learned to live with it. (Remember, living use always trumps a dead dictionary!)

If I tell my friend and helper, Gerardo, *"Necesito una pala."* ("I need a shovel.") He will invariably reply *"Ocupa una pala?"* ("You need a shovel?") He, and everyone else in the area, understand *necesito* just fine, but it is not the word they would normally choose to use on their own. I use the

---

42 "No one who knows Hebrew or another Semitic language could fail to be impressed by the Semitic tone and flavor of the New Testament and by its adoption of Semitic modes of speech" David Alan Black, *It's Still Greek to Me: An Easy-to-Understand Guide to Intermediate Greek* (Baker Academic, 1998), 150.

word that is more familiar to me as a cognate, but when they repeat me, they use words they are more comfortable with.

In the same way, we can see that the Jews preferred the Greek word *christos* because of its cognitive affinity to *meshiach* or *messiah*. Those more accustomed to Greek had no problem understanding that the word meant king even though it was not the word that they themselves would use as a first choice. This can be seen very clearly in Luke's record of Paul's experience at Thessalonica.

> Now when they had traveled through Amphipolis and Apollonia, they came to Thessalonica, where there was a synagogue of the Jews. And according to Paul's custom, he went to them, and for three Sabbaths reasoned with them from the scriptures, explaining and giving evidence tnat the Christ had to suffer and rise again from the dead, and saying, "This Jesus whom I am proclaiming to you is the Christ." And some of them were persuaded and joined Paul and Silas, along with a large number of the God-fearing Greeks and a number of the leading women. But the Jews, becoming jealous and taking along some wicked men from the market place, formed a mob and set the city in an uproar; and attacking the house of Jason, they were seeking to bring them out to the people. When they did not find them, they began dragging Jason and some brethren before the city authorities, shouting, "These men who have upset the world have come here also; and Jason has welcomed them, and they all act contrary to the decrees of Caesar, saying that there is another king, Jesus." (Acts 17:1–7)

The question needs to be asked; were the Jews guilty of

false accusation? Absolutely not! As soon as we understand that the word *Christ* in our English Bible is really a representation of a Greek word meaning "king," and is not just another name for Jesus, the passage makes perfect sense. If we translate instead of transliterate, verse three says that Paul was "explaining and giving evidence that the King had to suffer and rise again from the dead and saying 'This Jesus whom I am proclaiming to you is the King!'"

In this example it is clear that *christos* is understood to be synonymous with the Greek word *basileus*, the more typical word for king. In the following example we can see the exact opposite taking place:

> Now after Jesus was born in Bethlehem of Judea in the days of Herod the king, magi from the east arrived in Jerusalem, saying, "Where is He who has been born King of the Jews? For we saw His star in the east and have come to worship Him." When Herod the king heard this, he was troubled, and all Jerusalem with him. Gathering together all the chief priests and scribes of the people, he inquired of them where the Messiah was to be born. (Mat. 2:1-4)

Here we can see that, when the foreigners came speaking the *lingua franca* of the day, that no one had any trouble understanding them when they asked where the *basileus* was to be born. When they spoke among themselves, however the Jews used the word *christos*.

What is amazing about this passage is that those updating

my beloved NASB have replaced the transliteration of *christos*, found in previous editions, with the transliteration of *messias*, an Aramaic word not even found in the text. You decide, which makes more sense in the context, and seems more true to the intention of the Ambassador Matthew—*Christ*, *Messiah* or *King!*

A TITLE IN ANY ORDER

There remains but one more possible hurdle to our understanding of the Greek use of *christos* as king, and that is the flexibility of word order in Greek, as apposed to English. In order to see this most clearly we only need to point out several uses of *basileus* in Dr. Luke's account of Paul's audience before King Agrippa and his wife Bernice, recorded in Acts 25 and 26.

In Acts 25:13, we are introduced to the king as "*Agrippas o Basileus,*" which is literally "Agrippa the king." In verse 24, he is simply "*Agrippa Basileu,*" or "Agrippa King." And in verse 26, he is referred to as "*Basileu Aggrippa,*" which is "King Agrippa."

All you need to note is that in every one of these verses, the translators correctly and consistently used "King Agrippa" in their English translations. In the Greek text we often find constructions which would translate directly as "our Lord Jesus King," which is admittedly awkward English. It is perfectly legitimate, in such cases, to rearrange the words into a form more comfortable to the more rigid demands of our English grammar, as in: "our Lord, King Jesus," or to add the article, as in; "our Lord, Jesus the King."

This flexibility in the Greek language means that there may be times in which *christos* appears in the same construction that could also be used for a name. The mere fact that we can find a use in which *christos* could be used as a name does not mean that it is. George King of England, and George, King of England, have two distinct meanings in English, distinguished only by a comma.

For example, in the passage above "Agrippa *Basileu*," or "Agrippa King," could indeed be someone's name, if it were ever demonstrated that *basileu* was used as a surname in the same way that *chrestos* was. Even if this were to happen, it would be illegitimate in this passage to transliterate *basileu*, and thus turn it into a name. Remember, it is legitimate and expected that names be transliterated, but titles should always be translated.

To close this chapter, I can only restate my contention—that in *every* occurrence of *christos* in the New Testament, it was the author's intention that it be understood as the title *king*, and that *christos* was *never* understood as a name![43]

---

[43] I am dismayed that a number of dear evangelical friends who, after initially declaring that it is "of course ridiculous" to consider *christos* as a name rather than a title, have now recanted. It seems that once they saw the conclusions I have reached, they considered it less ridiculous than consistently rendering *christos* as king.

Four

WHAT DO YOU THINK?

"Elijah came near to all the people and said, "How long will you hesitate between two opinions? If the LORD is God, follow Him; but if Baal, follow him." But the people did not answer him a word." —I KINGS 18:21

If you've reached this point, you have already waded through a lot of difficult material. And quite frankly, you may have found it a bit difficult to swallow.

I have made the audacious claim that our beloved and authoritative New Testament has, through translation, been corrupted to the extent that the favored title of our Lord—of our King—has been removed from its pages and, all too often, from our vocabulary.

Of course, true followers of our king understand that He is

never caught unawares, in spite of the fact that history is full of examples that seem, at first glance, to indicate otherwise. As you might expect, I believe that there are other examples of this semantic subversion found in the scriptures, and intend to deal with many of them in the future.

Before proceeding, however, we need to deal with a few issues.

A Trivial Truth?

First, it is important to recognize that the failure to translate the word *christos* has not deprived us of the truth that Jesus is our king. One only needs to open any hymn book to see that, as noted earlier, the Holy Spirit has spread this truth abroad in our hearts.

On the other hand, this is not to say that the evisceration of meaning from *christos* has not been without effect.

Perhaps the loss of our sense of Jesus' kingship has historical parallels. For instance, in the dark days preceding Luther's rediscovery of the truth of God's grace, the Holy Spirit was still operating, and God had His faithful people. But I hope few would deny that the clear proclamation of the good news that followed his church-door posting of the 95 theses has been even more potent, thanks to the clarity with which it has been presented since that time.

Secondly, it should be understood that it is all too easy to read material such as this book out of idle curiosity, without making any sort of commitment to the claims being made. To those of you who find yourselves in this camp, I have a word—beware! Ultimately, what is being said here is either true or false. If it is false you need to stop reading it now, or at least read it with the intention of arming yourself to combat its falsehood and to warn others of its deception.

Great claims require great evidence, and I have tried to present just that. I have been trying to be meticulously (if not boringly) detailed in making my case. While there is still much to present and applications to be made, it is unlikely you will gain much by reading future installments unless you are already sympathetic to the case being made.

If what you are reading here is true, it is certainly more than a simple piece of trivia. Yet, if you do find yourself leaning in the direction of these claims, I am quite sure the enemy's next tactic will be to minimize them as trivial. I suspect he has invested too much perpetrating this deception to give up without a fight.

If you find yourself startled by what has been presented here, and yet you feel basic, if not total, agreement with what you have been reading, it is time to start asking yourself two questions.

One: how has my thinking—and more importantly, my behavior—been affected by my lack of understanding? As noted, our enemy has invested a lot of time and effort into obscuring the truth on this point; and I think it unlikely that he would do so without expecting big returns in the advancement of his cause.

The second question is, "Why me?" In other words, what purpose might God have in your discovery of these truths? I personally wrestle with this. I have no illusions that this will ever be a popular teaching, or even that what I am writing now will ever reach a wide audience. However, while I don't intend to limit God, I do think that He often chooses to work in understated, unexpected ways. When Gideon's army was too big, God proceeded to whittle it down. So I ask: why has our Lord allowed *you* to stumble across this obscure but important information?

TESTING OUR THESIS

With this background, it is finally time for you to make your own evaluation of how our case works out, scripturally.

In the verses listed below, the Greek word *christos* has been replaced with a blank space. You will note that I have included a broad spectrum of references spanning the entire New Testament, with special emphasis on what is unquestionably the latest inclusion—the aptly named "Revelation of Jesus Christ."[44] (If there really is any trend toward using *christos*

---

44 Does the use of "Christ" here, clarify or obscure the message of this book?

as a name it should be most evident here!)

Also, I am adding *the,* in those places where the Greek article occurs in association with the word *christos* in the original, so that you may realistically feel you are in a translator's position of deciding whether it should be included or excluded.

Remember too that you may have to add a direct or indirect article (*the* or *a/an*) if you believe the English warrants it.

Some may accuse me of "cherry picking" the verses which most clearly point to the kingship of Jesus. Perhaps I should plead guilty to the charge, and yet I can only point out that there are many, many "cherries" in the New Testament orchard!

Here are the translation options for *christos* as they have been laid out to this point:

- A word transliterated from the Aramaic: *Messiah*
- A word transliterated from the Greek: *Christ*
- The English denotation of the above words: *Anointed*
- The English connotation of Messiah in the Pentateuch: *Sanctified*
- The English connotation of Messiah used after the Pentateuch: *King*
- The academic view, Jesus' second name, aka *Mr. Christ*

When you fill in these blanks, simply ask yourself, honestly, which of these options make the most sense for filling in the blank. This is not an attempt at arm twisting, and I am not trying to force you to agree with me, though I obviously hope you will. This is an attempt to illustrate very clearly some of what I believe has been lost by the English use of the name Christ, and what can be gained by translating *christos* as king.

1. "Where is He who has been born King of the Jews? For we saw His star in the east and have come to worship Him." When Herod the king heard this, he was troubled, and all Jerusalem with him. Gathering together all the chief priests and scribes of the people, he inquired of them where the _____ was to be born. (Mat. 2:3-4

2. In the same way the chief priests also, along with the scribes, were mocking Him among themselves and saying, "He saved others; He cannot save Himself. Let this _____, the King of Israel, now come down from the cross, so that we may see and believe!" Those who were crucified with Him were also insulting Him. (Mark 15:31–32)

3. Demons also were coming out of many, shouting, "You are the Son of God!" But rebuking them, He would not allow them to speak, because they knew Him to be the _____. (Luke 4:41)

4. "Look, He is speaking publicly, and they are saying nothing to Him. The rulers do not really know that this is the _____, do they?" (John 7:26)

5. And according to Paul's custom, he went to them, and for three Sabbaths reasoned with them from the scriptures, explaining and giving evidence that the _____ had to suffer and rise again from the dead, and saying, "This Jesus whom I am proclaiming to you is the _____." ...and Jason has welcomed them, and they all act contrary to the decrees of Caesar, saying that there is another king, Jesus. (Acts 17:2, 3, 7)

6. Paul, a bond-servant of _____ Jesus, called as an apostle[45], set apart for the gospel of God, which He promised beforehand through His prophets in the holy scriptures, concerning His Son, who was born of a descendant of David according to the flesh. (Romans 1:1-2)

7. For as in Adam all die, so also in the _____ all will be made alive. But each in his own order: _____ the first fruits, after that those who are

---

45 We will see in a future work why *apostle*, another word transliterated from the Greek, is best translated as ambassador.

of the _____ at His coming, then comes the end, when He hands over the kingdom to the God and Father, when He has abolished all rule and all authority and power. For He must reign until He has put all His enemies under His feet. (1 Corinthians 15:22-25)

8. Therefore we also have as our ambition, whether at home or absent, to be pleasing to Him. For we must all appear before the judgment seat of the _____, so that each one may be recompensed for his deeds in the body, according to what he has done, whether good or bad. (1 Corinthians 5:9-10)

9. There is neither Jew nor Greek, there is neither slave nor free man, there is neither male nor female; for you are all one in _____ Jesus. (Galatians 3:28)

10. So then you are no longer strangers and aliens, but you are fellow citizens with the saints, and are of God's household, having been built on the foundation of the apostles[46] and prophets, _____ Jesus Himself being the corner stone. (Ephesians 2:19-20)

11. So that at the name of Jesus EVERY KNEE WILL BOW, of those who are in heaven and on earth and under the earth, and that every tongue will confess that Jesus _____ is Lord, to the glory of God the Father. (Philippians 2:10-11)

12. For our citizenship is in heaven, from which also we eagerly wait for a Savior, the Lord Jesus _____; who will transform the body of our humble state into conformity with the body of His glory, by the exertion of the power that He has even to subject all things to Himself. (Philippians 3:20-21)

13. For in Him all the fullness of Deity dwells in bodily form, and in Him you have been made complete, and He is the head over all rule and authority; and in Him you were also circumcised with a circumcision made without hands, in the removal of the body of the flesh by the circumcision of _____. (Colossians 2:10-11)

14. When He had disarmed the rulers and authorities, He made a public display of them, having triumphed over them through Him. Therefore no one is to act as your judge in regard to food or drink or in respect to a festival or a new moon or a Sabbath day—things which are a mere shadow of what is to come; but the substance belongs to _____. (Colossians 2:15, 17)

---

46 See previous note.

15. Nor did we seek glory from men, either from you or from others, even though as apostles of _____ we might have asserted our authority. (1 Thessalonians 2:6)

16. I charge you in the presence of God, who gives life to all things, and of _____ Jesus, who testified the good confession before Pontius Pilate,[47] that you keep the commandment without stain or reproach until the appearing of our Lord Jesus _____, which He will bring about at the proper time—He who is the blessed and only Sovereign, the King of kings and Lord of lords, who alone possesses immortality and dwells in unapproachable light, whom no man has seen or can see. To Him be honor and eternal dominion! Amen. (1 Timothy 6:13-16)

17. Suffer hardship with me, as a good soldier of _____ Jesus. No soldier in active service entangles himself in the affairs of everyday life, so that he may please the one who enlisted him as a soldier. (2 Timothy 2:3-4)

18. I solemnly charge you in the presence of God and of _____ Jesus, who is to judge the living and the dead, and by His appearing and His kingdom: preach the word; be ready in season and out of season; reprove, rebuke, exhort, with great patience and instruction. (2 Timothy 4:1)

19. Looking for the blessed hope and the appearing of the glory of our great God and Savior, _____ Jesus, who gave Himself for us to redeem us from every lawless deed, and to purify for Himself a people for His own possession, zealous for good deeds. (Titus 2:13-14)

20. So also the _____ did not glorify Himself so as to become a high priest, but He who said to Him, "YOU ARE MY SON, TODAY I HAVE BEGOTTEN YOU:" just as He says also in another passage, "YOU ARE A PRIEST FOREVER ACCORDING TO THE ORDER OF MELCHIZEDEK." (Hebrews 5:5-6)[48]

21. For if the blood of goats and bulls and the ashes of a heifer sprinkling those who have been defiled sanctify for the cleansing of the flesh, how much more will the blood of the _____, who through the eternal Spirit offered Himself without blemish to God, cleanse your conscience from dead works to serve the living God? (Hebrews 9:13-14)

---

47 What was His confession before Pilate?

48 Unlike Uzziah, Melchizedek was both a king and a priest. Also remember the context of the first O.T. quote.

22. But sanctify the _____ as Lord in your hearts, always being ready to make a defense to everyone who asks you to give an account for the hope that is in you, yet with gentleness and reverence. (1 Peter 3:15)

23. For we did not follow cleverly devised tales when we made known to you the power and coming of our Lord Jesus _____, but we were eyewitnesses of His majesty. (2 Peter 1:16)

24. Whoever believes that Jesus is the _____ is born of God, and whoever loves the Father loves the child born of Him. (I John 5:1)

25. Now to Him who is able to keep you from stumbling, and to make you stand in the presence of His glory blameless with great joy, to the only God our Savior, through Jesus _____ our Lord, be glory, majesty, dominion and authority, before all time and now and forever. Amen. (Jude 24)

26. Then the seventh angel sounded; and there were loud voices in heaven, saying, "The kingdom of the world has become the kingdom of our Lord and of His _____; and He will reign forever and ever." (Revelation 11:15)

27. Then I heard a loud voice in heaven, saying, "Now the salvation, and the power, and the kingdom of our God and the authority of His _____ have come, for the accuser of our brethren has been thrown down, he who accuses them before our God day and night." (Revelation 12:10)

28. Then I saw thrones, and they sat on them, and judgment was given to them. And I saw the souls of those who had been beheaded because of their testimony of Jesus and because of the word of God, and those who had not worshiped the beast or his image, and had not received the mark on their forehead and on their hand; and they came to life and reigned with the _____ for a thousand years. (Revelation 20:4)

29. Blessed and holy is the one who has a part in the first resurrection; over these the second death has no power, but they will be priests of God and of the _____ and will reign with Him for a thousand years. (Revelation 20:6)

Are you singing yet?

Five

WHAT'S THE BIG DEAL?

"Do not conform to the pattern of this world, but be transformed by the renewing of your mind. Then you will be able to test and approve what God's will is—his good, pleasing and perfect will." –ROMANS 12:2

In the last chapter I alluded to the fact that, even though our Lord has allowed the enemy an apparent victory in obscuring the meaning of *christos* in the New Testament, He has, at the same time, preserved our basic understanding that Jesus is our king. Because of this, some people think that any significant potential damage due to the misuse of *christos* as a name has been eliminated.

"What's the big deal?" they say. "This translation issue isn't all that critical. After all, I *know* He is my king."

Unfortunately, this dismissal has the effect of reducing the truth we have been expounding to a piece of trivia, and, in very important areas, makes the truth of scripture all but unintelligible. Are we really prepared to say that the authors of the New Testament would not care if we replaced their use of "King Jesus" with "Jesus of Nazareth" or "Mr. Christ?"

Does our perspective of the person of Jesus, and of His role and His work, really matter?

Remember how, in chapter three, we discussed the fact that everyday language habits of biblical translators trumped their scholastic acumen. Even though these godly men understood the rules of Greek grammar and the rules governing the use and non-use of the Greek article, they seem to have been incapable of applying this knowledge to the word *christos*.

We need to either conclude that this translation issue is the subconscious result of mental habits that confuse the Greek word with its false English cognate, Christ; or we must believe that they are intentionally doing violence to the Word of God.[49] And though violence is clearly being done, I prefer to think that it is the result of our enemy's trick rather than the scholars' ill will. And if these learned and God-fearing men are susceptible to this sleight of hand, what hope do the rest of us have of escaping the same?

The answer, of course, is the same for us as it is for them: we need to renew our minds in accordance with the truth.

---

49 Yes, the capitalization and the pun are intentional.

RETAKING THE TERRITORY

I believe a critical step toward this renewal of thought is to make a concerted effort to replace incorrect and thoughtless speech with what we know to be correct. If you recognize that Christ is not His name, and that king is His legitimate, true title, then begin speaking accurately—He is King Jesus, not merely "Jesus Christ."

Admittedly, this may seem difficult at first, and will certainly raise some eyebrows. However, I also submit that the very difficulty of this slight change is evidence of its necessity.[50]

As an incentive for you to make this vocabulary shift, I would remind you that the kingly meaning of *christos* is easily confirmed in any translation of the Bible, in any language, and without recourse to the original languages.[51] In other words, the idea is not completely strange to Christian conversation, even though the title has been all but lost.

Ultimately, though, I believe that the long ignorance of the actual meaning of *christos* testifies to the determined efforts of dark spiritual forces to maintain the status *quo*. This, in and of itself, should motivate us to change. If our enemy has invested concerted effort into veiling such a simple, confirmed fact, and if our flesh rebels so forcefully against

---

50 Some people and groups find this truth much more difficult to accept than others. I suggest that the more difficult an exercise, the greater the potential benefit from its practice.

51 It was not until *after* making this discovery that I began to study Greek.

such a simple change of speech; then we must surely press on to unveil the truth they fear.

That said, perhaps the simplest way to introduce a correct use of the text is to add the word *the* to the title *Christ* in your reading—at least if it feels more comfortable for you that way.[52] I did this myself for several years before becoming comfortable enough with the Greek to appreciate the depth and beauty of what our King's ambassadors had embedded in the text. While not a perfect solution, this usage is better than allowing the transliteration of *christos* to continue to obscure the authors' intent.

The second step I propose, though, is even more radical and, as such, even more basic: we *must* begin to reclaim the integrity of the message of our scriptures. In other words, we must, beginning with ourselves, deliberately undo the violence that has been done to the message of the Word by the veiling of Jesus' kingship.

Ideally, this would include more accurate Bible translations. Yet I am not holding my breath waiting for translators to wake up and say "Of course! How could we have missed such a simple thing; let's correct it immediately!" It may be years if ever before we see a New Testament translation that effectively incorporates this critical truth into its pages.[53]

---

52 You can find a list of all the occurrences of *christos* in the New Testament, along with whether or not the article is included, and my suggested translation on my blog: http://RadicalFish.net.

53 I have made some preliminary efforts in this direction which, Lord willing, will be presented in my next work.

So how are we to proceed?

Again, I submit that we need to develop the habit of verbally replacing the word *Christ*, even in our Bible reading and study, with the word *king*.

But I also submit that we need to begin to *think* differently about what is really being communicated within many of the biblical verses that use the title *christos*.

This mental and verbal clarification is an admittedly difficult task, but a critical one, I feel. It is in the scripture that we find everything we need to know about Jesus' life and ministry. It is in the scripture that we find the instructions necessary for life and godliness. And it is in the translations of the original scripture that we find this obscuring work of the slanderer.

We must begin to undo that work!

Reviewing our Problem

In the last chapter you were introduced to some basics of how to recapture the language and understanding that was originally intended. In the process, you should have begun to glimpse what all you have been deprived of by the enemy's sleight of hand.

You should also have seen that simply replacing occurrences of *Christ* with *King*, is not always an easy task and can lead to some very awkward readings. There are two basic reasons for this.

The first and most easily dealt with reason, has already been mentioned in chapter three—word order. In English usage, titles almost always precede names. In Greek usage, in contrast, word order is used for emphasis. Writing *King Jesus* placed more emphasis on His role as King, while writing *Jesus King* placed more emphasis on His person.

It is these kinds of subtle distinctions which demonstrate the prime advantages of learning the original language of the New Testament, as these nuances are difficult to carry over into English. The accepted convention among translators is to follow the grammatical demands of English rather than the subtleties of Greek. Consider the eleventh verse of Philippians, which was submitted for your examination in chapter four:

> "...so that at the name of Jesus EVERY KNEE WILL BOW, of those who are in heaven and on earth and under the earth, and that every tongue will confess that Jesus Christ is Lord, to the glory of God the Father." (Phil. 2:10-11)

It is easy to see that Paul is emphasizing that it is a specific person—Jesus, the king—who will be confessed as Lord. On the other hand, in the seventeenth verse we find that it is the kingship of Jesus which is being emphasized as the causative factor under consideration:

Suffer hardship with me, as a good soldier of Christ Jesus.
No soldier in active service entangles himself in the affairs
of everyday life, so that he may please the one who enlisted
him as a soldier. (2 Tim.2:3–4)

I am sure that you will agree that the ease and clarity obtained by on-the-fly replacing of both "Christ Jesus" and "Jesus Christ" with "King Jesus," more than make up for the subtle loss of the Greek nuance of emphasis. Still, though, if one is so inclined to preserve the word order, they can read "Jesus the king." It is these kinds of tradeoffs that translators need to deal with on a regular basis.

All of this brings us to the second and more difficult problem we confront in trying to undo the obfuscation found in the New Testament translations. Since the vast majority of us Christians are not equipped to read the Greek text directly, we are at the mercy of translators' willingness to communicate the Greek article. In the verses cited in the last chapter, I made a point of providing that information for you.

The authors of the New Testament were very precise in their use of the article, and this ultimately has great bearing on how the text is translated. In fact, I would submit that the translator's disregard of the basic rules for the use and non-use of the article in reference to *christos* is a prime factor in our misunderstanding of the New Testament teaching concerning His kingship.

The use and non-use of the article is technical and beyond the scope of this present work. I hope to deal with the issue in the future. In the meantime, permit me to give just one example of the type of subtle but significant differences that proper use of the article can lead to:

> ...*that at that time you were without* **Christ**, *being* aliens *from the commonwealth of Israel and strangers from the covenants of promise, having no hope and without God in the world. But now in* **Christ Jesus** *you who once were far off have been brought near by the blood of* **Christ**. *(Eph. 2:12–13 NKJV)*[54]

You will note that none of the three occurrences of *christos* are translated with the article, and we have no way of knowing whether or not it is present in the Greek text. It turns out that it is included at the last occurrence, resulting in the following reading:

> ...*that at that time you* were *without* **a king**,[55] *being aliens from the commonwealth of Israel and strangers from the covenants of promise, having no hope and without God in the world. But now in* **King Jesus** *you who once were far off have been brought near by the blood of* **the King**. *(Eph. 2:12–13, from NKJV)*

---

54 Scripture taken from the New King James Version˚. Copyright © 1982 by Thomas Nelson, Inc. Used by permission. All rights reserved.

55 When the article is absent in Greek, it is often necessary to add the English indirect article a/an. The guidelines for this are too complex to deal with here.

Note how, in the first translation given, the three bold selections could easily be replaced with "Jesus of Nazareth" with no loss of meaning, because in English they are simply transliterations, referring to His person and ignoring His position.

In the second variant, however, we actually translate *christos,* and also deal with the article and its absence according to the standard principles of translation. The message we discover here is not only subtly different, but also much more informative. In fact, we find that Paul's first use of *christos* in these verses is not even speaking directly of Jesus. Instead, he is emphasizing the fact that these people had no legitimate king whatsoever! Next he shows that their hope is restored by a specific king—Jesus. He concludes by stating that they have been brought into God's kingdom by the blood of *the* king who was just mentioned.

Verses like these demonstrate how we've been robbed of a great resource, thanks to the enemy's success in this area. To close this entire discussion, I would like to concentrate on three passages to fully illustrate the extent to which using the word *Christ* instead of translating *christos*, has completely eviscerated the significance of the authors' words.

YOU MUST BE BORN AGAIN

> *Whoever believes that Jesus is the Christ is born of God,*
> *and whoever loves the Father loves the child born of Him.*
> *By this we know that we love the children of God, when we*
> *love God and observe His commandments. For this is the*
> *love of God, that we keep His commandments; and His*
> *commandments are not burdensome. For whatever is born*
> *of God overcomes the world; and this is the victory that*
> *has overcome the world—our faith. (1 John 5:1-5)*

In this case, John's meaning in the Greek was so evident that the translators had no choice but to include the article on this occasion. There can be no doubt at all that John did not intend for *christos* to be understood as a name here.

Yet, just what *does* the first verse mean? What does a person believe when they believe that Jesus is the Christ? Obviously, it must be important, since being "born of God" is conditioned upon it.

Would it make sense to say, "I believe that Thomas is the Jefferson?" Yet, this is essentially how everything from English dictionaries to New Testament Greek reference books would have us understand the phrase "Jesus is the Christ."

When I ask people to define the message of verse one in their own words, I am almost inevitably told that "we must believe in Jesus Christ to be born again." Here again we see how mental habits trump one's understanding of grammar. "Jesus is the Christ" becomes reduced to simply *Jesus Christ*—a name!

It is all too easy to forget that, as it is used in English, Christ is merely a *name*. As noted in chapter three, English dictionaries define Christ as Jesus of Nazareth, and Greek reference books and common usage merely confirm this fact. It does us no good to simply try to think that the English *Christ* means king, because it does not. Instead, the Greek word *christos* means king. *Christ,* as the word has been transliterated and used in English, is a name. You and I are simply incapable of changing over 500 years of English usage.

In the introduction I said the church has been deceived— that she does not know what she has been saved from, or for. We emphasize salvation from sin, and salvation for eternal life. The enemy, while annoyed at these truths, would rather have us park here than realize the full truth: We have been delivered from the kingdom of darkness and have been transported into the kingdom of light in order to reign with our sovereign.

Listen again to John's words: "Whoever believes that Jesus is the King is born of God..." What does that last part, "born of God," actually mean? We are inclined to think that it means we will go to Heaven when we die. But the context doesn't mention Heaven; instead, it speaks of obeying his commands and overcoming this world. This is kingdom talk—not religion—for this life, not merely the next.

Remember Nathanael's confession from back in chapter

one? "Teacher, You are the Son of God; You are the King of Israel." Remember that his brother Philip had introduced Jesus as the son of Joseph? And remember that we discussed the fact that *son of god* was an ancient idiom for "divinely appointed ruler?" Well, here it is again.

If we unpack the words we find here and listen to them in a first century context, we find that John is saying; "Whoever believes that Jesus is the King is a divinely appointed ruler... and His commandments are not burdensome. For whatever is born of God (divinely appointed to rule) overcomes the world; and this is the victory that has overcome the world—our conviction that He is King and that we reign with Him." Wow!

This is an amazing revelation! Being "born again" means being "born of God." And being born of God means being His child; being His child means being a divinely appointed ruler!

You can almost hear the awe in the apostle's words: "Behold what manner of love the Father has bestowed upon us that we should be called the sons of God!" Adam, our progenitor, was created to rule over creation and was called the son of God. In his fall he lost the right to rule. Jesus, our older brother, has restored that right by His obedience. This is what it means to be joint heirs with the King! Is it any wonder that the accuser and his minions quake at the thought of God's people waking up to this truth and walking in it?

All of which brings us to our next passage...

CAN YOU PASS THE TEST?

> *Beloved, do not believe every spirit, but test the spirits to see whether they are from God, because many false prophets have gone out into the world. By this you know the Spirit of God: every spirit that confesses that Jesus Christ has come in the flesh is from God; and every spirit that does not confess Jesus is not from God; this is the spirit of the antichrist, of which you have heard that it is coming, and now it is already in the world. You are from God, little children, and have overcome them; because greater is He who is in you than he who is in the world. They are from the world; therefore they speak as from the world, and the world listens to them. We are from God; he who knows God listens to us; he who is not from God does not listen to us. By this we know the spirit of truth and the spirit of error. (1 John 4:1-6)*

Please notice the profound difference in the spiritual litmus test as we read it here, and how I am saying it *should* be read. Are we to ask if Jesus Christ came in the flesh, or if King Jesus did so? I submit it makes a big difference.

Though it is somewhat difficult to talk about, I have had more than one occasion to deal directly with demonic activity. Both I and others can testify to the fact that it is not terribly uncommon to encounter an unclean spirit that has no problem confessing that "Jesus Christ has come in the flesh."

The standard explanation I have heard dismisses these spirits as liars. One counselor I heard went so far as to say that demons are such liars that time should not be wasted by confronting them with this test. What good is a lie detector test that can be lied to?

However, the fact of the matter is that demonic spirits have no problem recognizing that a man you call Jesus Christ walked the earth 2,000 years ago—they were there. What they refuse to acknowledge is that He is their King.

Another interesting thing that we see in this passage is the spirit of antichrist. While this may be slightly off topic, it bears noting that *anti* in the Greek does not mean "against," but "instead of." When a Greek king would go off to battle, he would often leave a son or trusted friend in his place as the "anti-king." Since we have a living, vital, ongoing relationship with our Lord, we have no need of an anti-king.

I leave it to you, gentle reader, to discern who these many anti-kings are whom the world is listening to, and of whom John warns us.

When in Rome... Do as the Christians

When the message of Jesus first reached the town of Thessaloniki in southeastern Europe, its carriers were described as those "who have turned the world upside down."

Why was that? What was it about the message that was

so disturbing? For that matter, why was Jesus crucified? It is easy to forget that the Roman Empire was very diverse and accepting when it came to matters of religion, and made a habit of incorporating the faiths of conquered peoples into their own.

Many critics of Christianity today make the case that various cults extant in the Roman Empire were so clearly similar to Christianity, that early followers of Jesus were simply copycats. Yet the Romans seemed to have had no problem with the cults of Mithra and Dionysus, the two groups most often cited by opponents as the source of many Christian beliefs. If they were as similar as the critics claim, why did Rome have problems with the one and not the others? Even the Jews, as long as they were not engaged in active rebellion, were granted religious freedom under the Caesars.

The fact of the matter is that Rome, up until the fourth century, had little interest in regulating theology or religious belief. Nonetheless, they certainly had a problem with Christianity and its founder. The obvious question remains—*why?*

There certainly seems to be a disconnect between our understanding of Jesus' teaching and that of His first-century followers. As Philip Yancey said, "How would telling people to be nice to one another get a man crucified? What government would execute Mister Rogers or Captain Kangaroo?"[56]

---

56 Philip Yancey, *The Jesus I Never Knew* (Zondervan, 2008)

The flip side of this puzzle is seen in 2 Timothy 3:12, where Paul tells us "Indeed, all who desire to live godly in Christ Jesus will be persecuted." My friend, Finny Kuruvilla, sagely points out concerning this verse that according to the rules of formal logic, if a statement is true, its contra-positive must *necessarily* be true. (For example, if we accept the truth of the statement "all living cats breathe" we are required to accept the truthfulness of "if it doesn't breathe, it's not a living cat.") Hence, if we accept the truth of Paul's statement above, we must accept its contra-positive: if you do not suffer persecution you are not living godly in Christ Jesus.

Now, while I am willing to grant that Paul may be stating a general principle as opposed to a logical premise, the fact remains that the lifestyle lived by most who call themselves Christians today would not have resulted in their persecution in Paul's day. This leads us to the discomforting proposition that what commonly passes for Christianity today, may, in reality, have more in common with the Roman cults of Mithra and Dionysus than it does with its first-century namesake. We do well to ask, "Why *did* Rome persecute Christians?"

The answer turns on precisely the point we have been discussing. If, in an alternate universe, BDAG[57] had been correct, and *christos* had been understood as *Chrestos*—the name "Good," by non-Jews—Jesus would not have been crucified.

---

57 Walter Bauer, *A Greek-English Lexicon of the New Testament and Other Early Christian Literature*, 1st ed. (University Of Chicago Press, 2001). See chapter three.

But in *this* universe, the Romans clearly understood *christos* and its significance. Rome repeatedly demonstrated its tolerance of strange religions, including those that recognized mortals becoming gods, virgin births, and the dead being resurrected. They also repeatedly demonstrated their intolerance of any one claiming to be a king, and who did not pay tribute and worship to Caesar. And worship, by the way, is not acknowledging divinity; it *is* recognizing *sovereignty*![58]

This, of course, is the solution to the conundrum we have been considering. It is no great hermeneutic feat to recognize that Rome crucified Jesus because of His claim to be king. The charge was posted over His head, after all. What is often overlooked, however, is that it is precisely because of their allegiance to that king—Jesus—that Rome persecuted His followers.

That the God of the Jews should father a son with magical powers was no more offensive to the Romans than the idea that Zeus should father Hercules. But what *was* intolerable was the fact that Jesus' followers did not stop with recognizing Him as divine; they had the audacity to claim He was their actual sovereign.

---

58 We will spend considerable time discussing this in a future work.

In short, while the Jews preserved their religion by shouting, "We have no king but Caesar," the early Christians sealed their fate by unabashedly declaring, "We have no king but Jesus!"

Confirmation of this thesis can be found in John chapter 11, right after the account of the resurrection of Lazarus. Here we find the chief priests and Pharisees were very concerned over the increasing popularity of Jesus. Unlike other occasions, however, their contention was not over the blasphemous nature of Jesus' teachings, but over their potential political repercussions.

Note that they were not concerned that the people would believe Jesus or His teaching. But they were concerned that the people would believe *in* Jesus, and that this would invite Roman wrath. They said, "If we let him go on like this, all men will believe in Him and the Romans will come and take away both our place[59] and our nation."

Now this phrase "believe in Jesus" has a very modern ring to it, being heard in innumerable sermons every week, but what does it really mean?

In current parlance, "believing in Jesus" seems to be understood as believing that Jesus actually existed as a historical person; or, slightly better, believing that He died to save you from your sins so you could go to Heaven. Clearly, neither of these approaches makes any sense in this passage. No

---

59 Most modern translations interpret rather than translate this word and render it "temple." I think this is reasonable.

one was doubting the actual existence of Jesus and, at this specific time, He hadn't even died yet. More to the point, why would either of these beliefs cause a problem for the Roman Empire?

In order to understand this original sense of "believing in Jesus," we need to back up a bit and first consider this word *believe*.

First, it needs to be recognized that, in both English and Greek, *believe* is a verb that pairs with the noun *faith*. To believe is to have faith, and vice versa. Today, the word *believe* has degenerated to the point that it is commonly understood to mean accepting something without evidence, or even in spite of evidence to the contrary, as in: "I know it looks bad, but we just have to *believe*." In Greek, however, the word is related to the idea of being convinced or convicted. It means to accept something *because* of the evidence.

In addition to this, we discover distinct political overtones in the words *faith* and *believe,* both in the society of Jesus' day, and in ours as well. Consider the motto of the U.S. Marine Corps: *Semper Fidelis*, "Always Faithful."

In like manner, Caesar demanded that his subjects be faithful—that is, that they give him their unreserved allegiance. He demanded that his subjects believe in him, and as long as this was proffered, he could overlook all manner of impropriety, "Serve whatever gods you will, but recognize *me* as sovereign."

This insistence was the basis of the chief priests' and Pharisees' extreme discomfort. It was one thing to think that Jesus was a blasphemer, or a pretender to the people's affections; it was something completely different to be afraid that He would bring the wrath of Rome down on their heads.

It seems that the fears of the chief priests and Pharisees were well founded. In the very next chapter we find Jesus entering the capital, Jerusalem, to the adulation of her people who shout, "Hosanna! Blessed is He who comes in the Name of the Lord, even the King of Israel." John goes on to tell us that this was in fulfillment of the scripture: "Fear not daughter of Zion; Behold, your King is coming, seated on a donkey's colt." Interestingly, he also makes clear that it was the resurrection of Lazarus that set this ball in motion.

Yancey[60] was right—you don't crucify someone for telling people to be nice to one another, or even for following directions to be nice. You get crucified for claiming to be king. It is not merely desiring to live godly that warrants persecution; it is desiring to live godly *in King Jesus* that does so. This is what it means to believe in Jesus, and this is what Rome could not tolerate!

All of this begs the question: would the Romans have viewed you as an adherent to just one more of many religions, or would they have understood that you were following a

---

60 Yancey, *The Jesus I Never Knew.*

completely different king?

Would the Romans have found you worthy of crucifixion?

Do you believe in King Jesus?

ALL HAIL THE POWER OF JESUS' NAME!

by Edward Perronet

All hail the power of Jesus' Name!
Let angels prostrate fall;
Bring forth the royal diadem,
And crown Him Lord of all!

Ye chosen seed of Israel's race,
Ye ransomed from the fall,
Hail Him Who saves you by His grace,
And crown Him Lord of all!

Let every kindred, every tribe,
On this terrestrial ball,
To Him all majesty ascribe,
And crown Him Lord of all!

Oh, that with yonder sacred throng
We at His feet may fall!
We'll join the everlasting song,
And crown Him Lord of all!

AFTERWORD

"You can't accurately see until you abandon your worldview. Your worldview is incredibly useful In everyday life—it's the set of assumptions, biases, and beliefs you bring to the interactions you have with the world, and it saves a lot of time. Because you don't have to come to new conclusions after each interaction, it's easier to process familiar inputs and easier to be consistent. But your world view, by its nature, keeps you from seeing the world as it is. " —SETH GODIN, *THE ICARUS DECEPTION*

Thank you for taking the time to read this work!

I realize simply reading it may have been a challenge. I also recognize that even more important work is now ahead of you. You must now prayerfully consider whether what you have read is truth or a deception. If you believe it is not true, I cannot help but believe it must be hard to "kick against the pricks." But then, maybe I am mistaken, and maybe I need kicking.[61] Please contact me through the RadicalFish.net

---

61 ☺

blog—I would love to hear from you.

On the other hand, if it is truth, you face the challenge of determining how to walk it out. I have given you some hints, but I cannot give you full answers as to why the King has set you on this path of rediscovering the significance of His kingship, or where it could lead. I think, however, that I can assure you that it will ultimately be more glorious than difficult—and yes, it will be hard.

I am hesitant to suggest that our paths might be joined for a bit more than only the reading of this book. I have started a blog with the purpose of spreading the news of our King, and providing support for those who are seeking to be faithful to Him. There is much work to be done in the cause of the King, and I humbly invite you to help spread the good news of His Kingship.

If this little book has been of benefit to you, please share it, tell others about it, and comment on our blog at http://RadicalFish.net. If it looks like something that might help you in your walk with God, please sign up for our newsletter, leave a comment, and participate in the discussion. Lord willing, there are other books I believe I am to write, and you will be able to find out about them there.

Whether you like this book or not, please write a brief review at http://www.amazon.com/dp/B00CW512ZS. If you think it is deceptive, you owe it to your Lord to warn people of its danger. But if it helped you in some way, a five-star review will help others find it.

I have made what some might consider the ludicrous decision not to copy protect the electronic version of this work with DRM. My King, not my wits nor the law, is my defender. If you believe that this work would help someone you know, and neither of you can afford it, please feel free to make a copy, or contact us through http://RadicalFish.net for a free one. However, please remember a workman is worthy of his wages, and I trust you will compensate me and my family with your prayers for support and protection in this work.

More than all else, please pray that we all be faithful to our Lord, King Jesus, and that we would be willing to do whatever He asks, whatever the cost. "And whatever you do, whether in word or deed, do it all in the name of the Lord Jesus, giving thanks to God the Father through him."[62] Now to the King eternal, immortal, invisible, the only wise God, be honor and glory forever and ever. Amen."[63]

As I stated earlier, proceed in His favor, secure in His love, with eyes wide open, seeking His Truth.

Favor and peace in Him Whom we serve,

Christopher Gorton

---

62 Colossians 3:17
63 1 Timothy 1:17

APPENDIX

In chapter three I shared my incredulity at the scholarly contention that the use of christos in the New Testament was gradually converted from a title to a name. I pointed out that, based on what we find in translations, no such transition is seen. Rather we find that translators universally transliterate christos as a name. They only include the author's use of the Greek article the when it is absolutely unavoidable to do so.

I have searched extensively to find a justification for this claim of transition, but without avail. I have found it repeated in many scholarly works and texts, but always without references or arguments to support the claim.

The closest I have come to finding a justification is the following list of scriptures which BDAG[64] cites, presumably to show this transition occurring. As noted in chapter three, any hope of seeing a chronological progression in usage is immediately dashed due to the fact that the verses are placed in order of occurrence in the New Testament, not in actual chronological order.

We are further disappointed when we find that in all but one occurrence *christos* is accompanied by the article *the* which, in all but one case, does not appear in the translation.

Given that this is the only argument I could find in favor of this thesis, it seems appropriate to dedicate this appendix to its rebuttal. You will find each of these verses listed below, along with the article in parentheses where it is found in the text.

In each case the translation is from the NASB, and the use of the article is taken from the *SBL Greek New Testament*[65] text. I have left *christos* transliterated as *Christ*, and will leave it to your judgment to determine if this makes sense, and if you can see a transition from its use as a title to that of a name.

64 Bauer, *A Greek-English Lexicon of the New Testament and Other Early Christian Literature*, 1091.

65 Michael W. Holmes, *The Greek New Testament: SBL Edition* (Society of biblical Literature, 2010).

Matthew 11:2

Now when John, while imprisoned, heard of the works of (the) Christ, he sent *word* by his disciples and said to Him, "Are You the Expected One, or shall we look for someone else?"

Acts 8:5

Philip went down to the city of Samaria and *began* proclaiming (the) Christ to them.

Acts 9:20

And immediately he *began* to proclaim Jesus in the synagogues, saying, "He is the Son of God."

Note: The inclusion of this reference is puzzling. Few translations even included the word Christ in this verse: however, several texts have "τον χριστον" in place of Jesus. Verse 22 makes very clear that no use as a name can be inferred here.

Romans 9:3, 5

For I could wish that I myself were accursed, *separated* from (the) Christ for the sake of my brethren, my kinsmen according to the flesh... whose are the fathers, and from whom is the Christ according to the flesh, who is over all, God blessed forever. Amen.

1 Corinthians 1:6, 13, 17

...even as the testimony concerning (the) Christ was confirmed in you... Has (the) Christ been divided? Paul was not crucified for you, was he? Or were you baptized in the name of Paul?... For (a) Christ did not send me to baptize, but to preach the gospel, not in cleverness of speech, so that the cross of (the) Christ would not be made void.

Note: Three of the four references to *christos* in these verses are accompanied by the article *the* which was omitted by the translators. In the third case, where the ambassador omitted the article, the rules of Greek grammar require us to add the indirect article a. In a future work we will see that at the time, the word "gospel" had specifically royal overtones.

1 Corinthians 9:12

If others share the right over you, do we not more? Nevertheless, we did not use this right, but we endure all things so that we will cause no hindrance to the gospel of (the) Christ.

1 Corinthians 10:4, 16

...and all drank the same spiritual drink, for they were drinking from a spiritual rock which followed them; and the rock was (the) Christ... Is not the cup of blessing which we bless a sharing in the blood of (the) Christ? Is not the bread which we break a sharing in the body of (the) Christ?

2 Corinthians 2:12

Now when I came to Troas for the gospel of (the) Christ and when a door was opened for me in the Lord...

2 Corinthians 4:4

...in whose case the god of this world has blinded the minds of the unbelieving so that they might not see the light of the gospel of the glory of (the) Christ, who is the image of God.

Galatians 1:7

...which is *really* not another; only there are some who are disturbing you and want to distort the gospel of (the) Christ.

Galatians 6:2

Bear one another's burdens, and thereby fulfill the law of (the) Christ.

Ephesians 2:5

...even when we were dead in our transgressions, made us alive together with (the) Christ (by grace you have been saved)...

Ephesians 3:17

...so that (the) Christ may dwell in your hearts through faith; *and* that you, being rooted and grounded in love...

EPHESIANS 5:14

For this reason it says, "Awake, sleeper, and arise from the dead, and (the) Christ will shine on you."

PHILIPPIANS 1:15

Some, to be sure, are preaching (the) Christ even from envy and strife, but some also from good will;

COLOSSIANS 1:7

just as you learned *it* from Epaphras, our beloved fellow bond-servant, who is a faithful servant of (the) Christ on our behalf...

COLOSSIANS 2:17

...things which are a *mere* shadow of what is to come; but the substance belongs to (the) Christ.

2 THESSALONIANS 3:5

May the Lord direct your hearts into the love of God and into the steadfastness of (the) Christ.

1 TIMOTHY 5:11

But refuse *to put* younger widows *on the list*, for when they feel sensual desires in disregard of (the) Christ, they want to get married...

Hebrews 3:14

For we have become partakers of (the) Christ, if we hold fast the beginning of our assurance firm until the end,

Hebrews 9:28

...so (the) Christ also, having been offered once to bear the sins of many, will appear a second time for salvation without *reference to* sin, to those who eagerly await Him.

1 Peter 4:13

...but to the degree that you share the sufferings of (the) Christ, keep on rejoicing, so that also at the revelation of His glory you may rejoice with exultation.

2 John 9

Anyone who goes too far and does not abide in the teaching of (the) Christ, does not have God; the one who abides in the teaching, he has both the Father and the Son.

Revelation 20:4

Then I saw thrones, and they sat on them, and judgment was given to them. And I *saw* the souls of those who had been beheaded because of their testimony of Jesus and because of the word of God, and those who had not worshiped the beast or his image, and had not received the mark on their forehead and on their hand; and they came to life and reigned with (the) Christ for a thousand years.

I cannot think of a better verse on which to close this book. Here, at the end of the last book in the New Testament, written in the closing years of the first century we see a clear and glorious declaration of the *christos*—not as a name—but borne as a regal title by the lamb who was slain.

ALL HAIL THE SLAUGHTERED LAMB!

THE GOD OF ABRAHAM PRAISE

by Thomas Olivers

The God of Abraham praise, who reigns enthroned above;
Ancient of everlasting days, and God of Love;
Jehovah, great I AM! by Earth and Heav'n confessed;
I bow and bless the sacred Name forever blessed.

The God of Abraham praise, at Whose supreme command
From Earth I rise—and seek the joys at His right hand;
I all on Earth forsake, its wisdom, fame, and power;
And Him my only Portion make, my Shield and Tower.

There dwells the Lord our King, the Lord our righteousness,
Triumphant o'er the world and sin, the Prince of peace;
On Sion's sacred height His kingdom still maintains,
And glorious with His saints in light forever reigns.

The God Who reigns on high the great archangels sing,
And "Holy, holy, holy!" cry, "Almighty King!
Who was, and is, the same, and evermore shall be:
Jehovah—Father—great I AM, we worship Thee!"

Before the Savior's face the ransomed nations bow;
O'erwhelmed at His almighty grace, forever new:
He shows His prints of love—they kindle to a flame!
And sound thro' all the worlds above the slaughtered Lamb.

The whole triumphant host give thanks to God on high;
"Hail, Father, Son, and Holy Ghost," they ever cry.
Hail, Abraham's God, and mine! (I join the heav'nly lays,)
All might and majesty are Thine, and endless praise.

Notes:

Made in the USA
Charleston, SC
16 August 2013